D1729488

Olayiwola Bello

Mobile Telecommunication Customer Loyalty in Nigeria

Determining factors

Diplomica® Verlag GmbH

Bello, Olayiwola: Mobile Telecommunication Customer Loyalty in Nigeria: Determining factors, Hamburg, Diplomica Verlag GmbH 2012

ISBN: 978-3-8428-8473-1
Druck: Diplomica® Verlag GmbH, Hamburg, 2012

Bibliografische Information der Deutschen Nationalbibliothek:
Die Deutsche Nationalbibliothek verzeichnet diese Publikation in der Deutschen Nationalbibliografie; detaillierte bibliografische Daten sind im Internet über http://dnb.d-nb.de abrufbar.

Die digitale Ausgabe (eBook-Ausgabe) dieses Titels trägt die ISBN 978-3-8428-3473-6 und kann über den Handel oder den Verlag bezogen werden.

© Diplomica Verlag GmbH
http://www.diplomica-verlag.de, Hamburg 2012
Printed in Germany

DEDICATION

To

Me, Myself and I

ACKNOWLEDGEMENT

For a long time to come, I know how much I owe to my indefatigable supervisor, Dr. C. J. Agorzie whose instructions and constructive criticisms saw me through this work. I have learned quite a lot from him and certainly will learn yet more, I am very grateful for all of this.

My profound heart of gratitude and sincere appreciation also goes to KKK, Naeem Balogun and my other colleagues at the University of Ilorin for their support, inspiring encouragement, illuminating advice and various kinds of help. With a lot of gratitude, I recognize the loving support of Janet Bewaji, Adewale Shonekan, Tunde Sanni, Shakirah and Tessy. My sincere appreciation also goes to my Uncle, Abd'Wahab Bolaji who has always been there for me through thick and thin. To my mum and sister I say thank you very much for always believing in me and making me believe more in myself.

Ultimately, I thank Allah, the Almighty God who sustained me to the completion of this work despite all the seeming obstacles. His joy is and will always be my stronghold.

TABLE OF CONTENT

LIST OF TABLES

LIST OF FIGURES

ABSTRACT

This work sought to assess and analyze the variables capable of influencing loyalty of mobile phone subscribers as well as how service providers can enhance loyalty of their customers in Nigeria. The study was basically a survey that used the quantitative approach. A structured questionnaire was developed and personally administered to a sample of University of Ilorin students across four major GSM operators in the country. Four hundred (400) respondents were sampled through a stratified random sampling. Out of this, three hundred and forty-eight (348) copies of the questionnaire constituting 87% response rate were got for analysis. Of the eleven (11) operational factors that were used to assess loyalty of customers in the Nigeria Mobile Telecoms industry, all variables except Brand Image and Service Centre Quality were found to be capable of influencing customer loyalty and also considered as the most important loyalty variables in the industry. The unavailability of Mobile Number Portability was found to be a prominent factor in tying consumers down to service providers while the generally low satisfaction with the present state of service delivery in the industry also plays a role in this direction. Therefore, the retention been enjoyed by the service providers can be described as circumstantial. Part of the recommendations given include the service providers embarking upon drives that will reduce to its barest minimum drop calls, improve call quality and SMS delivery which is likely to make subscribers perceive given quality as high among others

CHAPTER ONE

1.1   Background

With the increasing competition in the market, customer loyalty has become a decisive factor in long-term business profits. At its high, customer loyalty connotes the high entry barriers for the competitor to enter the market, and it significantly contributes to reduction in marketing costs. Attracting new customers requires a company to invest quite much time and money and this process always span a long period of time associated with uncertainties and risks.

The number of loyal customers as a sign of market share is more meaningful and significant than the total number of customers. More loyal customers translate to high profits. Loyal customers will continue to purchase or receive the product or service from the same enterprises and they will be willing to pay higher prices for the quality products and first-class services, thereby increasing sales revenue. From the afore mentioned, the focus of many enterprise managers at this point is on marketing management aspects to improve customer loyalty in order to gain the competitive advantage in the face of fierce competition. The importance of customer loyalty has been identified by many researchers and academicians in different commercial enterprises in years past (Ahn, 2006; Gerpott el al, 2001; Lee 2001). This importance in no doubt does not exclude the telecommunication industry and by extension the Nigerian telecoms industry.

Nowadays, as the mobile telecommunication market is being saturated, the growth rate won't be higher than it used to be some times ago. The situation makes mobile telecommunication companies not only to promote their service quality, but also change their marketing core strategy from expansion to holding their existing customers by enhancing and optimizing the customers' loyalty. (Long-Yi Lin & Jen-Chun, 2004)

Telecommunication industry is a very typical industry, customer's importance to enterprises, and how to attract, develop and maintain customers has became more and more important in the sharp internationalized mobile telecommunication competitions. The issue of how to improve customer loyalty is a very important for mobile communication operators. Therefore, customer loyalty is playing a significant role in the telecommunication market competition because it has become a critical variable in the fight for survival among telecom operators.

Research has shown the importance of loyal customers in business enterprises and not excluding the telecom sector. The facts presented by Schmidt (2006) go as follows:

The typical company gets 65% of its business from its existing customers.

- It costs 5 times more to find a new customer than to keep an existing customer happy.
- It takes 12 good service experiences to overcome a single bad one.
- 7 out of 10 customers who switch to the competition do so because of poor service
- 91% of unhappy customers won't buy again from the company that displeased them
- And unhappy customers will not only defect, they will grumble to 9 of their friends.

He however continued by writing that:

If an enterprise is rated by a customer as five on a scale of one to five, such customer is six times more likely to return than if the enterprise rating is four. Also, dissatisfied customers whose complaints are taken care of are very likely to remain loyal, and often become "customer advocates" if you go out of your way to fix their problem. All these are pointing to the fact that attending to the needs, satisfying and gaining the confidence of customers breed loyalty and in the long run increases the net worth of an enterprise.

Customer loyalty is one of the most domineering factors that drive the profits of the operators in the telecom industry (Ramneck & Preety, 2009). Loyalty programs or drive towards ensuring customer loyalty are capable of stabilizing market because loyal customers are less sensitive to price. The more stable the market the higher the profit margins (Muller, 1998). We think customer loyalty is very important in mobile telecom industry and hence, the need for the variables relating to it to be understood.

1.2 The Characteristics of Nigerian Mobile Telecom Market

A large, evolving and profitable market

Nigerian Mobile Telecom market is indeed the fastest growing market in Africa, maintaining its lead with active subscribers of about 78 million (NCC, March 2010) and relegating South Africa to second place with about 45 million subscribers. Nigerian telecoms came into mainstream in 2001 when the deregulation of the subsector of the economy gave way to private involvement. The telecommunication system was opened up with the issuance of Global System for Mobile communication (GSM) unified license in 2001. GSM license in Nigeria cost about US$285million. Nigerian Telecommunication (NITEL) was the only operator in the market before 2001 with subscribers of about 500,000 from a population of about 140 million. The deregulation ushered in telecom players like MTN, Glo Mobile, Zain formerly Celtel, Etisalat, Visafone, Multilinks, Starcomm and Zoom formerly Reltel. The telecom regulator in Nigeria is Nigerian Telecommunication Commission (NCC), with reference to NCC Act 2003; 3-(1) "There is established of a commission to be known as Nigerian Telecommunications Commission with responsibility for the regulation of the telecommunication sector in Nigeria".

The market is divided into urban and semi-urban, and rural market. Tele density in the urban is about 65% while semi urban is about 45% and rural is less than 15%. Product Segmentation is GSM and Code Division Multiple Access (CDMA). (www.ncc.gov.ng, March 2009)

Major Players

MTN, Zain, Glo and Etisalat control the GSM market. While Visafone, Multilinks, Starcomm and Zoom formerly Reltel are in the CDMA product segment. The market shares of these major mobile telecoms are MTN-40.54%, Zain- 30.20%, Glo Mobile- 28.11 and Etisalat- 0.7%, M-Tel Mobile phone business of NITEL-0.45%. While Visafone leads the CDMA market, follow by Multilinks, Starcomms, and Zoom. (www.ncc.gov.ng, March 2009)

The Growth Progression

From a bit above 500,000 NITEL fixed wire line and mobile subscribers in 2001. The industry grew to over 7million subscribers in 2004; in December 2008 the subscribers in the market grew to 62.99million. An addition of 22.59 million subscribers in 2008 alone represented 56% annual growth rate. Recent figure as at January 2009 put the subscribers' base at 64.16. While GSM subscribers are in the range of 57million, CDMA subscription in Nigeria grew from just 380,000 in 2007 to more than 6million at the end of 2008. The country intelligent report on Nigeria by Pyramid research (2009) stated that the market grew by 23% with total industry revenue of US$8.42billion. With mobile penetration of 42% revenue will increase to US$11.14billion by 2013 with forecasted annual increase of 5.7%. The telecom market has been named the largest mobile market in Africa. Tele density of 0.73% in 2001 has steadily increase over the year to 33.72% as at December 2006 and about 45% aggregate in December 2008. The current market installed capacity is 117.892 million as at December 2008. The mobile industry ARPU (Average Revenue per User) in 2003 was around US$54 per month but

15

as at 2008 December was US$13. (www.ncc.gov.ng, March 2009).

It is however expected that ARPU will continue to fall with competition, and also as the service providers dig deeper into the lower strata of the society in villages to explore the ever ready market available naturally by the country's population strength

- Mobile number portability (MNP) does not exist in the Nigerian mobile telecoms market.

Mobile number portability (MNP) is the ability that enables mobile telephone users to retain their mobile telephone numbers when changing operators. Many countries are MNP countries for example, USA, Sweden, Denmark, Germany, Korea, UK, Turkey etc. But till now, Nigeria does not have MNP, so if a subscriber wants to change from one operator to another, he or she has to worry about a plenty of trouble after using a new cell phone number, like to inform every contact, miss a lot of phone calls and so on.

- Majority consumers buy handsets by themselves.

Before Third Generation (3G), Global System for Mobile Communications (GSM) and Code Division Multiple Access (CDMA) are the two main network technologies. The CDMA operators require proprietary handsets that are linked to one carrier only. But for GSM, Subscriber Identity Module (SIM) card itself is tied to the network of an operator, rather than an actual phone. So operators, who use CDMA, always sell mobile service together with a handset while business model of operators who use GSM is to sell SIM card to their customers. The majority of subscribers in Nigeria are using GSM, that is to say, operators only sell SIM card to their customers and their customers buy cell phone separately. So the willingness to switch cell phones would not be an issue that makes customers change operators as long as they are in GSM network.

1.2.1   The Current situation of Nigerian Mobile Telecom Industry

There are about fourteen mobile operators in the Nigerian mobile telecom industry, they are: MTN, Globacom, Zain, Etisalat, Visafone, EMTS, M-Tel, Multi-Links, Starcomms, Reliance, M-Tel, Zoom, Intercellular and Onet. These operators not only supply the basic mobile voice services but also value-added services such as data, IP telephone and multimedia, though the bulk of their service is around voice and text

All the operators are privately owned with the exception of M-tel that has government stake and it is also been touted for privatization. However, regulation of the sector rests on a government agency in the name of National Communication Commission (NCC).

16

Though controlled by the same department of the government, competition between the operators is serious and very fierce.

1.3   Statement of the Problem

Research into what factors impact on customer loyalty has been carried out in other countries such as South Korea, Germany, and France and so on. Gerpott (2001) considers the network quality, which is reflected in excellent indoor and outdoor coverage and in the clarity of voice reproduction without any connection break-downs; the price paid for obtaining access to and using the network; the quality of the exchange of information between customer and supplier (1) in response to customer (telephone) enquiries and (2) in the course of interactive activities initiated by the network operator (e.g., presentation of an invoice) have an important impact on customer loyalty in Germany market. Lee (2001) thinks pricing, area coverage, clarity of sound, access to provider, precision of billing service and perceived difficulty to switch are the main factors which have important impact on customer loyalty in France. Ahn (2006) considers that call drop rate (percentage of abnormally terminated calls), the number of complaints, monthly billed amounts and customers with a non-use or suspended status are positively associated with the probability of customer churn in South Korea mobile telecom industry.

From the review of literature above, we find that different countries have different factors that affect their customer loyalty in the mobile telecom market. Comparing with the other mobile telecom market situation, the Nigerian market is a different one (in terms of structure, status and market saturation) and thus the need to understand the peculiarities of factors on which the loyalty of mobile telecom users hinge on. As earlier stated that different countries have different factors that affect their country's customer loyalty in the mobile telecom market, thus, Nigeria as the most populous African country and indeed a force to be reckoned with in the World League of Nations when it comes to population is not unlikely to have different factors that affect mobile telecom customer loyalty. Hence addressing questions like what factors affect the loyalty of customers in Nigeria's Mobile Telecoms industry and how has operators fared on these factors will be of importance in this thesis.

1.4 Research Questions

The purpose of this work is to find out what kind of specific and concrete operational factors have important impact on Nigeria mobile telecom customers' loyalty. The questions to be addressed by his study include:

- What factors have important impact on customer loyalty in Nigeria telecom industry?
- What is the performance of the service providers collectively on these aspects?
- How can service providers map out better ways of enhancing customer loyalty?

1.5 Objectives

The overall objective of this work is to gain a better understand of the variables that affect the loyalty of customers/users of mobile telecommunication service as provided by the service providers.

The specific objectives are to:

(i) Investigate which factors specifically affect the loyalty of mobile telecom users.

(ii) Investigate the performance of the telecom service providers against the identified factors.

(iii) Determine how service providers can better enhance the loyalty of their customers.

1.6 Justification

The work is immensely significant in diverse ways to business/marketing practitioners, policy makers and stakeholders within the telecom sector. To the management of Nigeria's mobile telecom networks, the findings and results that will be reported in this study will provide a more reliable scientific measure and perspectives for describing and evaluating the variables that affect the loyalty of their customers towards the services they deliver. This will provide empirical support for management strategic decisions in several critical areas of their operations, and above all, provide a justifiably valid and reliable guide to designing workable service delivery improvement strategies for creating and delivering customer value, achieving customer satisfaction and loyalty, building long-term mutually beneficial relationship with profitable customers and achieve sustainable business growth in Nigeria.

To policy makers like government agencies such as the National Communication Commission (NCC), the finding and results of this study will provide invaluable insights and a more reliable guide to monitoring the impact of the operations of Nigeria's mobile telecom operators. It could also serve as a yardstick for measuring partly their respective policy goals and objectives. Particularly, it will facilitate immensely the National Communication Commission (NCC) in achieving some of its policy goals, which include: enhancing the reliability and efficiency in the provision of communication services.

1.7   Scope and Delimitation

The mobile telecommunication operators under review for this thesis are basically the GSM operators and these also exclude M-tel which at the time of this thesis is almost nonfunctional. Therefore the survey took a holistic look at the customer loyalty factors of the industry as a whole and not in any way attempt to single out a particular service provider. Data for the study was generated from questionnaire personally administered to carefully selected students of the University o Ilorin, Ilorin Kwara State.

CHAPTER TWO

2.1 Conceptual Framework

2.1.1 Customer Loyalty

Customer loyalty has been studied both in the academic field and real business world for years. To keep a long-term relation with their customers is one of the most important goals of many companies in the modern business world. The cost to keep existing customers is much cheaper than obtaining new customers. Rosenberg and Czepiel (1984) indicated that expense of keeping an existing customer is less than one sixth of winning a new customer. Customer loyalty now is one of the key factors can help a company win long-term success (Andres Kuusik 2007).

Customer loyalty can be classified into proactive loyalty and situational loyalty. Oliver (1999) suggested that proactive loyalty occurs when a consumer frequently buys a brand and settles for no other substitute while situational loyalty exists when the buyer purchases a brand for a special occasion. We can also classify customer loyalty into the behavior loyalty and the attitude loyalty. Behavior based customer loyalty focuses on the long-term choice probability for a brand, for example, repeat purchase probability, while, attitudinal loyalty focuses on brand recommendations, resistance to superior products, repurchase intention, and so on. (Xu-Xiaoli, Wan-Yinghong, Huan-Zhijian, Liu-Hui 2006)

- **Behavior Loyalty**

Many scholars (Ehrenberg, 1991; Soderlund, 1998; Ja-Shen Chen et al. 2006.) think loyalty refers to customer's consistent purchasing behavior. Jacoby and Kyner (1973) opined that customer loyalty is the behavioral outcome of a customer's preference for a particular brand from a selection of similar brands, over a period of time, which, importantly is the result of an evaluative decision-making process. But can we equate repurchasing activity of a customer of the same brand product to loyalty? Amine (1998) thinks that repurchasing under the two cases earlier outlined above can not be called loyalty purchasing:

(1) Consumers' repurchasing may be due to the consumers' tendency to reduce or avoid search efforts. There is a high probability of interrupting this consistent buying and switching to another brand at the first opportunity or inducement to do so (price increasing, new brand launching or brand out of stock). This kind of repurchasing can

be called inertia purchasing.

(2) When there is a narrow choice in a product category, the repeat purchasing improves too. This consistent brand buying may express more inertia or constrained repeated behavior rather than loyalty with commitment to that brand. Consumer commitment towards the purchase (behavior loyalty) of same brand doesn't mean he/she is a loyal consumer.

- **Attitudinal Loyalty**

What is attitudinal loyalty? Jacoby and Chestnut (1978) defined it as a customer's predisposition towards a brand. It is a function of psychological processes. Amine (1998) considers the commitment towards a brand as attitudinal loyalty. Baldinger and Rubinson (2001) also believe this kind of commitment is a dispositional commitment. Bandyopadhyay et al. (2007) think attitude strength of a brand is operationalized by the number of positive attributes associated with the brand. (A person has a stronger (or weaker) attitude toward a brand when he/she believes that the brand possesses more (or less) positive attributes.) While Rundle-Thiele (2005) use word of mouth as a measure of attitudinal loyalty.

- **Attitude-Behavior Loyalty**

Behavioral loyalty suggests that the repeat purchasing of a brand over time by a consumer expresses their loyalty, while the attitudinal perspective assumes that consistent buying of a brand is a necessary but not sufficient condition to 'true' brand loyalty (Amine 1998). Likewise Dick and Basu (1994) precisely suggested that a favorable attitude and repeat purchase were required to define loyalty. Behavior loyalty must be complemented with a positive attitude towards this brand to ensure that this behavior will be pursued further. Oliver (1999) defines loyalty as a deeply held commitment to re-buy or re-patronize a preferred product/service consistently in the future, thereby causing repetitive same-brand or same brand-set purchasing, despite situational influences and marketing efforts having the potential to cause switching behavior. Dick and Basu (1994) state that, "customer loyalty is viewed as the strength of the relationship between an individual's relative attitude and their repeat patronage".

In this research we define the loyal customer from two aspects: (1) repeat purchasing the same brand products (2) positive word of mouth. Both are indispensable. Here the word of mouth means the extent to which customers inform friends and family (Rundle-

Thiele, 2005). In this thesis, we agree with Butcher et al. (2001) view about positive word of mouth. They identify four variations of the concept of positive word of mouth: (1) providing positive word of mouth (2) recommending the service to others (3) encourage others to use service (4) defending the service provider's virtues

2.1.2 The Antecedents of Customer Loyalty

We think there are three factors that can lead to customer loyalty. The first one is customer satisfaction (Amine, A., 1998; Oliver, 1999; Butcher et al., 2001; Li Liu, 2008). Butcher say the increased loyalty results from high levels of customer satisfaction. The second factor is switching cost. Switching cost has a positive relationship with customer loyalty and Fornell (1992) stated that switching cost have impact on the connection between customer loyalty and satisfaction. The third one is the corporate image. Corporate image and customer satisfaction have mutual effect on each other. And in turn they both have impact on customer loyalty

Customer Satisfaction: Butcher et al. (2001) opined that increased loyalty results from high level of customer satisfaction. Oliver (1999) had earlier described it in a more figurative way: "satisfaction becomes transformed into loyalty much like a caterpillar becomes transformed into a butterfly. After this metamorphosis, the two creatures are not the same and share virtually no common characteristics except for their biological origins."

Switching Cost: Switching cost has to do with the aggregate of cost, both financial and non-financial related that a customer will consider before embarking on a move to dump a current product/service for a new one and this has to do with the intention of a customer willing to repurchase. Switching cost is positively related to customer loyalty and Fornell (1992) stated that switching cost have impact on the connection between customer loyalty and satisfaction.

Corporate Image: Corporate image and customer satisfaction have mutual effect on each other. And in turn they both have impact on customer loyalty. These factors are put into consideration in coming up with the model to measure loyalty.

2.1.3 Customer Loyalty: Does it Really Work?

There are large numbers of research on the function of customer loyalty. But does customer loyalty really work? Dowling and Uncles (1997) think loyalty is not working. Launching and maintaining loyalty programs cost firms money (Muller, E., 1998).

There are "Leaky Bucket Theory" and "Polygamous Loyalty" that exist in the market. The empirical record and the predictive norms show that only about 10 percent of buyers for many types of frequently purchased consumer goods are 100 percent loyal to a particular brand over a one-year period. Moreover, 100 percent loyal buyers tend to be light buyers of the product or service. Most of customers not only buy one brand (Polygamous loyalty). For example, surveys of European business airline travelers show that more than 80 percent are members of more than one airline loyalty scheme. Customers don't only loyal to one company (Ehrenberg et al. 1988).

However, in mobile telecom industry the situation is different. The multi-brand loyalty does not exist in the market. Usually one customer only chooses one mobile operator at one time. Once customers have been acquired and connected to a certain network of an operator, their long-term relations with the operator are settled. It is more important to the company's success than some other industry sectors (Gerpott et al. 2001). We are not sure the percentage of loyal customers in the whole customers but we know "80/20 law" (Dowling and Uncles, M., 1997). The 80/20 law states that about 80 percent of revenue typically comes from only 20 percent of customers. With such a skewed distribution of customers, it makes sense to concentrate most marketing resources on the 20 percent. Most of these customers are loyal customers.

Loyalty programs can stabilize market because loyal customers are less sensitive to price. The more stable the market the higher profit margins (Muller, E., 1998). We think customer loyalty is very important in mobile telecom industry.

2.1.4 New Trend of Customer Loyalty

There are several levels of customers (Cary, W. and Adams, A. 2009):

1. Dissatisfied customer--Looking for someone else to provide product or service.

2. Satisfied customer---Open to the next better opportunity.

3. Loyal customer--Returns despite offers by the competition.

Nearly two decades after loyalty theories radically changed the business world, the balance of power has shifted from companies to customer, now the market is more customer- oriented market, and customer loyalty is becoming more and more indispensable and important in the real market. Now more than ever, organizations need to understand the mechanisms of customer loyalty to profit from it (Cary, W. and Adams, A. 2009). As such, Jennifer Kirkby (2008) provides a trip through the history of customer loyalty and shows how we can learn from past mistakes and current thinking. Loyalty today is not what it uses to be.

Loyalty is more qualitative and subjective – it is a feeling of connection to, and belief in, a company and its proposition, created by a 'feel good' factor from interactions. Products with after-sales service no longer sufficed, the customers wanted better experiences with suppliers and had started to use the internet to advise each other on which companies to use: three-quarters of consumers would recommend their favorites company to others. So customer loyalty is different between industries. And it also has been added more meaning right now by the development of the technology (Jennifer Kirkby, 2008).

Five key loyalty-marketing trends are identified and explored in detail, while you think about customer loyalty; you might want to take the following five factors into considerations. (Michael T. Capizzi and Rick Ferguson, 2005)

---Ubiquity; Existence or apparent existence everywhere at the same time; omnipresence

---Technology enables but imagination wins. The ability to confront and deal with reality by using the creative power of the mind; resourcefulness

---Coalition lite; an alliance of people, factions, parties, or nations; a combination into one body; a union).

---Customer analytics; Division of a subject into elemental parts or basic principles; Using, or subjecting a subject to a methodology involving algebra or other methods of mathematical analysis; Proving a known truth by reasoning from that which is to be proved.

---the Wow! Factor wow

Used to expressing wonder, amazement, or great pleasure. This is the outstanding success.

2.2   Customer satisfaction

2.2.1   The Definition of Customer Satisfaction

As the key driver of customer loyalty, many researchers increased emphasis on customer satisfaction. High level of customer satisfaction may lead to more loyal customers which means can bring more profit for enterprise. There are many kinds of definition of customer satisfaction, but no precise definition has already been developed. Just like Oliver (1999) said the working of customer mind is like a black

24

box. That is an observer can only see what goes in and what comes out but not what happened inside. Satisfaction may result from a very simple or a complex process involving extensive cognitive, affective and other undiscovered psychological and physiological dynamics (Oh & Parks, 1997).

Comparing the definitions of satisfaction, it can be found that satisfaction is stated to be a relative concept always judged in relation to a standard (Yuksel Atila et al., 2001). That means if you define customer satisfaction on different angles, you can get different definition. Usually, many researchers conceptualize customer satisfaction as a personal feeling that customers compare perceived quality performance with expectations. This kind of conception is represented by Oliver's (1980) expectancy-disconfirmation framework. He states that customers compare the perceived quality of products and service with their prior expectations. The difference between expectations and perceived quality is called disconfirmation. If it is positive disconfirmation (the expectations are met or exceeded), the consumer is satisfied; if it is negative disconfirmation (perceived quality falls short of expectations), and then the customer is dissatisfied. The model was further developed by Anderson et al. (1993).

Some other researchers suggest that customer satisfaction can be defined at two levels (Bitner & Hubbert, 1994; Jones et al. 2000; Bodet, Guillaume, 2008). They are transaction-specific satisfaction and overall satisfaction (holistic). Transaction-specific satisfaction refers to the consumer's satisfaction with a discrete service encounter. It is based on the individual level; they base their judgment of customer satisfaction on a specific purchase occasion. Overall satisfaction refers to the consumer's overall subjective post-consumption evaluative judgment based on all encounters and experiences with particular organization. Wang, Yonggui et al. (2004) opined that overall satisfaction is more fundamental and useful than transaction-specific consumer satisfaction in predicting subsequent consumer behaviors and a firm's past, present and future performance. ACSI (American Customer Satisfaction Index), SCSB and ECSI define customer satisfaction as overall satisfaction. So here, our theoretical framework treats customer satisfaction as overall satisfaction.

2.2.2 The Definition of Perceived Quality of Products and Service

From the end of last century, companies already realized that understanding and meeting consumer's need is very important for their company. It can help companies get competitive advantages. Supplying high quality products and service seems very

25

important. Companies that have goods and services that are perceived as being of high quality typically have greater market share, higher return on investment, and higher asset turnover than firms which have goods and services perceived as being of low quality (Kim et al., 2004).

The definition of quality which we will use in our thesis refers to perceived quality. Because it was found that the objective quality concepts are not identical for managers, customers and researchers (Zeithaml 1988). We need a higher level abstract definition to describe the quality. Definition of perceived quality seems suitable under the situation. Zeithaml (1988) describes perceived quality as consumer's judgment about the superiority or excellence of a product or service. The perceived quality has two primary components of consumption experience (Fornell 1996):

(1) *Customization*, that is, the degree to which the firm's offering is customized to meet heterogeneous customer needs, and

(2) *Reliability*, that is, the degree to which the firm's offering is reliable, standardized, and free from deficiencies.

O'Loughlin (2004) thinks that there are two general kinds of conceptions of perceived quality: product quality (hardware) and service quality (software/humanware). Perceived product quality is the evaluation of recent consumption experience of products. Perceived service quality is the evaluation of recent consumption experience of associated services like customer service, conditions of product display, range of services and products etc.

2.2.3   Customer Loyalty and Perceived Quality

According to Ahn's (2006) research in Korea, call drop rate (percentage of abnormally terminated calls) has a significant impact on the probability of churn; however, the call failure rate (the percentage of calls that are not initiated due to interference or poor coverage) does not. While Gerpott (2001) considers the network quality, which is reflected in excellent indoor and outdoor coverage and in the clarity of voice reproduction without any connection break-downs, as one of the key drivers of customer satisfaction in Germany market. Lee (2001) thinks the quality of core services (coverage of the calling area and clarity of sound) is very important on customer satisfaction in France telecom market. There is no relative or similar research in Nigeria's Telecom Industry, but we think Nigeria telecom market is similar with others. That is the coverage of the area and call quality (clarity of voice) are key drivers of customer satisfaction. Customer satisfaction has a strong relationship with customer loyalty which has already been proved, so does coverage of the area and call quality (clarity of voice) have big importance on customer loyalty?

SMS play a great important role in telecommunication in the Nigerian setting. Though it might seem more pronounced amongst the educated younger generation. More people choose to send SMS to express their love to others, especially for young boys and girls. Usually, we will receive / send a lot of SMS during the festival to get / express wishes. The second reason is that text has a unique charm it can express something that the language may not express. The third reason is that young people are the main groups of SMS users and they like communicating via SMS not only because it's cheaper than the call, but also because they can send it every time in any places. For example, many students like to send SMS while classes are going on.

But usually one SMS only contain 160 characters which give a large limitation to mobile users in Nigeria when they send SMS. We also have problems relating to missing our SMS during the sending process, especially at the "peak time" (for example the festive periods). Going by the youth been a vibrant population of phone users it is important that this angle be investigated as this might have a strong relationship with customer loyalty.

In this thesis, the "network quality" refers to the internet connection and the speed to login website, received and send email etc. with cell phone. In 3G era, the quality of product for different telecom companies is largely dependent on the speed of internet. If the mobile operator can supply high speed mobile internet, it should be able to win more customers.

Nobody will deny that price is a key driver when people make a purchasing decision. Especially for the telecom industry, people usually store certain amount money in their account. So they will make balance inquiry from time to time: how much money already been consumed and how much left. If the inquiry system is not reliable, nobody will feel assured when they are consuming. So we want to know does the convenient and reliable inquiring balance system have a big importance on customer loyalty.

It's hard to find a mobile operators' service center on the street in western countries. This might not be unconnected with the fact that people are already used to dealing with most of their transaction through the internet and customer care line. But in Nigeria it is a different scenario. Most people still patronize the service centers.

Compared with service center, the customer care line service has some incomparable advantages.

(1) You can transact whenever (24 hours service) and wherever you like and the call is free.

(2) It can handle complaints.

In our pre-description, we know the importance of loyal customers for the firms. Its central role in maintaining customer loyalty clearly positions complaint handling as an important strategic tool for enterprises. Complaints represent an opportunity to remedy product or service related problems and to positively influence subsequent customer behavior. Dealing effectively with complaints can have a dramatic impact on customers' evaluations of the experiences for the encounter service as well as enhance their likelihood of repurchase and limit the spread of damaging negative word-of mouth (Blodgett, 1997). If a firm can deal efficiently with a customer's complaints with high quality, the complain customer can transfer into been a loyal customer. Nigerians no doubt like other people of the world like to use explicit way to express their mind and such is the same when they are complaining. While costumers will prefer to complain through the customer care line for the inherent advantage in it, the service quality delivered by the workers in the service center and hotline are very important. It might directly influence the consumers experience and affect the consumer overall satisfaction.

So in this thesis, we will like to investigate the effect of the service quality of service center and customer care hotline on customer loyalty. We treat the overall evaluation of the encounter service (face to face service, call hotline etc.) quality as perceived service quality.

2.2.4   The Definition of Perceived Customer Value

The market is driven by customers' demand. With advancements in science and technology, there is no great difference among the same category products. Many firms are transforming their focus from looking internally within the organization for improvement by way of quality management, downsizing, business process re-engineering or lean production and agile manufacturing to customers (Wang Yonggui, 2004). Customer value which has a significant impact on behavior intentions of customer has been considered as a successful factor for firms.

Like other definitions discussed before, there are many different expressions of the concept of perceived value. These definitions are very popular and already are widely used by many researchers in their research papers:

- Value is the consumer's overall assessment of the utility of a product based on perceptions of what is received and what is given. (Zeithaml 1988)
- Buyers' perceptions of value represent a trade-off between the quality or benefits they perceive in the product relative to the sacrifice they perceive for paying the price. (Monroe 1990)
- Customer value is market perceived quality adjusted for the relative price of your product. (Gale 1994)
- Customer value as a customer perceived preference for and evaluation of those product attributes, attribute performances, and consequences arising from use that facilitate achieving the customer's goals and purposes in use situations (Woodruff, 1997).

Comparing these definitions, we can find some consensus among them. There is some form of trade-off between what the consumer gives up (price, sacrifice) and what the consumer receives (utility, quality, benefits) (Doods, 1991; Woodruff, 1999; Kashyap & Bojanic, 2000). It implies at the same time that when consumers are able to practically evaluate trade-offs between price and quality, perceived overall value may provide the best summary evaluation of the experience (Kashyap, 2000). All the value is based on the customer's perspective. In this thesis, we adopt the definition of customer value as "the perceived level of product quality relative to the price paid" as defined by Fornell, (1996).

2.2.5 Customer Loyalty and Customer Perceived Value

When we talk about the value of products, a word usually appeared in our mind: "price". Price is often used by consumers as an extrinsic product-quality cue (Teas & Agarwal, 2000). Scitovszky (1945) observed that the use of price as an indicator of product quality is not irrational, but represents a belief that price in the marketplace is determined by the interplay of the forces of competitive supply and demand. Generally, people perceive price as just a number which present how much money you should pay if you want to get a product or service. That is what we called "actual price". But do consumers really remember the actual price of the products in their daily lives? Research has revealed that consumers do not always know or remember actual prices of

29

products. Instead, they encode prices in ways that are meaningful to them (Teas & Agarwal, 2000). This is what we usually called "perceived price". Zeithaml (1988) defined perceived price as "what is given up or sacrificed to obtain a product". Here what we give up can be money but can also be non-monetary things like time, convenience and search costs or a combination of some or all of them.

Just like we stated earlier, customer value is the comparison between perceived quality and perceived price. Comparing quality with price can balance the difference in income among people.

2.2.6 The Triad Relationship between Perceived Quality, Perceived Value and Customer Satisfaction, Customer Loyalty

Many previous studies measure customer satisfaction, perceived quality and customer value in a single item, but we think the single item study will lead to many shortcomings. Because all survey variables are believed to be measured with certain degree of errors (Fornell et al., 1996), single-item scales cannot assess or average out the variance due to random errors, specific items, and method factors (Yi, 1990). In contrast, some studies employing multi-item scales to measure perceived quality and consumer satisfaction show that multi-item scales are significantly more reliable than the single-item scales (Wang, 2004). In this thesis we treat customer satisfaction, perceived quality and customer value as a whole. As ACSI, SCSB informed, the relationship between perceived quality, perceived value and customer satisfaction, customer loyalty can be visualized as:

(1) Perceived Quality and Perceived Value have a direct and positive effect on customer satisfaction;

(2) Perceived Quality has a positive relationship with increase in Perceived Value and Customer Satisfaction.

(3) Perceived Quality and Value do not have a significant effect on customer loyalty.

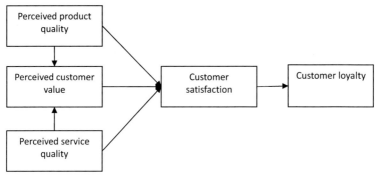

Figure 2.1: The Relationship between Quality, Value, Satisfaction and Loyalty

2.3 Switching cost

2.3.1 Definition and Typology

Switching cost is defined as the cost involved in changing from one service provider to another (Porter, 1980). He also argued that there are three types of switching cost: (1) procedural switching costs, primarily involving the loss of time and effort; (2) financial switching costs, involving the loss of financially quantifiable resources; and (3) relational switching costs, involving psychological or emotional discomfort due to the loss of identity and the breaking of bonds. Through his research, he proved that all the three types of switching cost have influence on consumers' intentions to stay with their current service provider, explaining more variance than satisfaction.

Jones et al., (2002) argued that switching cost is financial and psychological risk when a customer changes a provider. They proposed six dimensions of switching cost: (1) lost performance costs; (2) uncertainty costs; (3) pre-switching search and evaluation costs; (4) post-switching behavioral and cognitive costs; (5) setup costs; and (6) sunk costs.

Lost performance costs are perceptions of the benefits and privileges lost by switching. Uncertainty costs are perceptions of the likelihood of lower performance when switching. Pre-switching search and evaluation costs are perceptions of the time and effort of gathering and evaluating information prior to switching. Post-switching behavioral and cognitive costs are perceptions of the time and effort of learning a new service routine subsequent to switching. Setup costs are perceptions of the time, effort, and expense of relaying needs and information to provider subsequent to switching. Sunk costs are perceptions of investments and costs already incurred in establishing and maintaining relationship. By two studies, they proved that every one of the six dimensions is associated with repurchase intentions and indicates that lost performance costs and sunk costs are more strongly associated with repurchase intentions than others. (Jones et al., 2002)

Burnham, et al., (2003) defined switching costs as the onetime costs that customers associate with the process of switching from one provider to another. They provided eight dimensions of switching cost: economic risk costs, evaluation costs, learning costs, set-up costs, benefit loss costs, monetary loss costs, personal relationship loss costs, and brand relationship loss costs and then summarized these eight dimensions into three types: procedural, financial, and relational switching costs. Procedural switching costs: consisting of economic risk, evaluation, learning, and setup costs, this type of switching cost primarily involves the expenditure of time and effort. Financial switching costs: Consisting of benefits loss and financial-loss costs, this type of switching cost involves the loss of financially quantifiable resources. Relational switching *costs:* consisting of personal relationship loss and brand relationship loss costs, this type of switching cost involves psychological or emotional discomfort due to the loss of identity and the breaking of bonds. By their studies, they stated that all the three switching cost types appear to drive consumers' intentions to stay with their current provider.

2.3.2   Switching Cost and Customer Loyalty

According to the previous studies, switching cost is said to be the cost incurred when a customer changes product or service providers. No matter how switching cost is classified, in general business world it is related to a customers' intention to repurchase. In a critical look at the relationship between switching cost and customers' repurchase intention, anecdotal evidence suggest that these two shows a positive correlation; the higher the switching cost, the higher the customers' repurchase intention is. Repurchase intention is one aspect of attitudinal loyalty, which is one type of customer loyalty so switching cost can be said to have a positive correlation with customer loyalty in the general business world.

Switching cost also has influence on the relationship between customer satisfaction and customer loyalty. The level of switching costs moderates the link between satisfaction and loyalty (Jonathan et al., 2001). Fornell (1992) suggested that switching cost has impact on the relationship between customer loyalty and satisfaction. Jones and Sasser

(1995) noted that false loyalty increase when switching cost is high.

In the mobile telecommunication industry, switching cost play an important role in the customer loyalty. In telecommunication industry, once customers have been acquired and connected to a certain network of an operator, their long-term relations with the operator are more important to the company's success than some other industry sectors (Gerpott et al. 2001). In the mobile telecommunication sector, procedural switching costs can be embodied as time and effort spent on evaluating alternative operators, getting used to new service system and informing your contacts of the new number (if there is no mobile number portability).

Financial switching costs can be embodied as cost of new SIM card, financial loss on bonus and score accumulation, loss on prepayment (for prepaid customers). Relational switching costs can be embodied as emotional discomfort when facing the inconvenience, and loss of former relationship with staff and so on. Jones and Sasser (1995) noted that when false loyalty increases, switching cost is high. They suggest that when the switching cost is low, there are few false loyalties and satisfaction can easily keep customers to stay and dissatisfied customers can easily make the decision of changing a provider. On the contrary, when customers are facing high switching cost, customer satisfaction's influence are weaker; even if customers are dissatisfied with the products or service, they may still stay.

Serkan et al., (2005) stated that switching cost factor directly affects loyalty, and has a moderating effect on both customer satisfaction and trust and therefore, it plays a crucial role in winning customer loyalty. This conclusion is based on the research on the Turkey's mobile telecom market.

In addition to objectively measurable monetary costs, switching costs may also pertain to time and psychological effort involved in facing the uncertainty of dealing with a new service provider.

Kim et al. (2004) argued that factors creating switching costs positively affect customer satisfaction this conclusion is based on a survey in the Korea mobile telecommunication market. The authors embodied switching cost into sub factors.

(1) Loss cost: the perception of loss in social status or performance, when cancelling a service contract with an existing carrier.

(2) Adaptation cost: the perceived cost of adaptation, such as search cost and learning cost.

(3)Move-in cost: the economic cost involved in switching to a new carrier, such as the purchase of a new device and the subscriber fee. They also stated that losses involved in removing special customer status or customer benefit programs, and move-in costs such as changing numbers, could be an important switching barrier for customers changing to other service providers.

Jia and Yan (2005) tested what factors drive customer loyalty in the telecommunication sector in China by qualitative interview and questionnaire survey, and their findings is that customer loyalty is driven by customer satisfaction, trust relationship and switching cost synthetically. Switching cost has a stronger influence on customer loyalty than do customer satisfaction and relationship trust in the low stake holding condition. Which means when customers perceive low interests correlated with themselves of the service from a certain provider, switching cost plays a more important role in obtaining customer loyalty. In another research conducted in China by Yonggui Wang et al., they selected randomly 300 mobile telecommunication customers in two cities, Tianjin and Hohhot, to make questionnaire which focus on what factors can impact customer loyalty in the mobile telecom market. Their finding is that switching cost plays a moderating role in impacting process of customer loyalty (Yonggui et al., 2005).

Jonathan et al. (2001) suggested that, in mobile telecommunication sector, switching cost plays a significant moderating role in the satisfaction-loyalty link only for the economy and standard groups in which customers consider quality of core service very much when they are choosing operators. They also suggested that firms should provide consumption-based incentives such as free hours, added value, services, and lower, weekend pricing, a new handset with discounted price, and free value-added services for heavy users.

These researchers suggested that switching cost is an important factor that can affect customer loyalty in the mobile telecommunication sector. Researchers either tested the general switching cost or divide switching cost into mutable types and test type by type. But the types are only stay in the academic level, for example, financial switching cost, relational switching etc. Nearly none of them give us a conclusion that in empirical, or to say, in the real mobile telecommunication industry, what embodied form of switching cost have important influence on the customer loyalty. Some of the researchers use questionnaires in their studies; they choose questions related to score accumulation and frequent bonus.

Mobile number portability gives subscribers right to keep their phone number when they change service providers. The main purpose of number portability adoption is to

34

minimize the subscriber inconveniences associated with switching providers and to lower switching costs (Lee et al. 2006). However, in Nigeria number portability is yet to be introduced to mobile telecommunication, that is to say, when customers change to another operator, they are not allowed to retain their cell phone numbers. This may bring big inconvenience after switching to another operator because the customers have to inform all their contacts of the new number and people would still call the old number at the early weeks, thus the customers may miss some phone calls which may be vital.

2.4   Corporate Image

2.4.1   The definition of corporate image

MacInnis and Price (1987) described image as a procedure by which ideas, feelings, and previous experiences with an organization are stored in memory and transformed into meaning based on stored categories. Corporate image is described as the overall impression made on the minds of the public about a firm (Barich and Kotler, 1991). It is defined as perceptions of an organization reflected in the associations held in consumer's memory (Keller, 1993). As well, Nguyen and LeBlanc, (1998) defined corporate image as subjective knowledge, as an attitude, and as a combination of product characteristics that are different from the physical product but are nevertheless identified with the product.

Corporate image is the result of a process (MacInnis and Price, 1987). The process stems from ideas, feelings and consumption experiences with a firm that are retrieved from memory and transformed into mental images (Yuille and Catchpole, 1977). Customers can obtain it from their own experience, words of others, advertising and so on. Serkan and Gokhan concluded that corporate image stems from all of a consumer's consumption experiences, and service quality is a function of these consumption experiences. Hu et al. (2009) claimed that customers who received high service quality during service delivery would form a favorable image about the firm. Service quality has an indirect effect on corporate image.

2.4.2   Corporate Image and Customer Loyalty

Selnes (1993) stated that image should be incorporated into a model of loyalty together with satisfaction. Image and satisfaction, are associated with loyalty. Thomas et al. (2008) pointed that corporate image is an important factor for service companies because of its impact on loyalty. They argued that experience plays an important role in building customer loyalty, the corporate image for experienced customers, who have established a reliable image, become a strong predictor of loyalty. So for continuously provided services, most customers will be experienced and have a strong image; their image will be an important factor in building loyalty. Jay (2007) also claimed that corporate image is influenced both by service quality and customer satisfaction, which in turn influences customer loyalty.

In the sector of Mobile telecommunication, researchers also studied the impact of corporate image. According to a survey, which Nokia took 3,900 interviewees, corporate image with network quality, and switching barriers together are the factors that can keep current customers stay in the operator. Groholdt et al. (2000) stated that corporate image is an important driver of customer satisfaction and loyalty in the industries of soft drinks, banking and telecommunications. Liu (2008) in his study of Chinese telecommunication marketing opined that corporate image has a significant impression on services quality, customer value, customer satisfaction and customer loyalty. Similarly Chen, (2006) of the Taiwanese telecommunication sector observed that building up image is one of the important tasks to retain customers.

Nguyen and Leblanc (2001) stated that corporate image is related to the physical and behavioral attributes of the firm, such as business name, architecture, variety of products/services, and to the impression of quality communicated by each person interacting with the firm's clients. Except customer's experience, corporate image can be built by publicity and advertisements. Company can use these methods to foster a good and healthy company image for them. Andreasen and Drumwright (2001) argued that social responsibility plays an important role in increasing corporate image. Corporate social responsibility is defined as company's status and activities regarding its responsiveness to its perceived societal obligations (Brown and Dacin, 1997). Nowadays companies should not just chase interest, they should take over some social responsibilities to improve social welfare and protect the living environment of people. Customers will have a good impression of a company if it takes part in some charity events, treat their employees well, be ethical and obey laws when doing business. A good impression can lead to a high corporate image.

From the previous study of corporate image, we can come to the conclusion that, corporate image and customer satisfaction have mutual effect on each other. In turn they both have impact on customer loyalty. Many researchers stated that corporate image is a subjective impression to a firm and this impression is partly from the customers' consumption experiences. Service quality is one of the most important functions of the consumption experience. Service quality and other factors constitute customer satisfaction, so this can also improve that customer satisfaction and corporate image affect each other mutually. Besides consumption experience, customers can build their image about a firm from words from others, news of the firm, advertisements, business name and logo, corporate social responsibility.

In terms of mobile telecommunication sector, corporate image also have influence on customer loyalty. But researchers mainly focused on the general concept of corporate image, and not many of them have studied the embodied forms of corporate image and few more have a focus on the mobile telecommunication industry. We want to discover if some of the sub-factors or to say embodied forms of corporate image can have effect on customer loyalty in the Nigerian mobile telecommunication sector. From the foregoing, Corporate Image is influenced a lot by customer satisfaction and experience.

The sub-factors to be examined under Corporate Image are:

(1) Advertisements of corporate image;

(2) Corporate Social Responsibility.

These are two factors that have been mentioned in previous literatures.

2.5 Theoretical Framework

In this thesis, we will develop our own model of customer loyalty with respect to the peculiarities of the telecommunication industry. Our model is similar with ECSI (European Customer Satisfaction Index), but with some differences as discussed below.

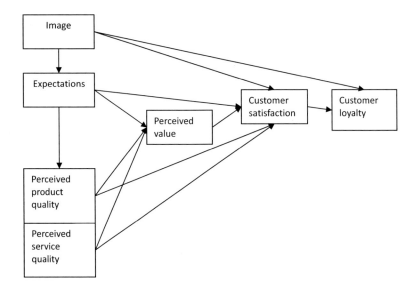

Figure 2.2: Source: European Customer Satisfaction Index (1999) as cited in Cassel, C., Eklof (2001)

1. In this study, the factor "expectations" is omitted from our model. In fact, expectations have an important role in the definition of customer satisfaction and perceived service quality. We do not consider the factor "expectations" based on following reasons:

(a) As we mentioned before, some researchers define customer satisfaction as the difference between the customers' perceived quality with expectations. There are also some researchers that define service quality as "the outcome of an evaluation process where the consumer compares his expectations with the services he perceived". That refers to the difference between expected service and perceived service (Parasuraman, 1988; Oh, H., 1999; Yuksel , 2001;Wang, Yonggui,2004; Ueltschy, 2007). From the foregoing, we can deduce that the concepts of customer satisfaction and service quality are almost the same. Although the researchers already made the distinctions between the two conceptions, they are still easily confused.

(b) Based on the "gap" definition of service quality, Parasuraman (1988) developed a SERVQUAL model to measure service quality. This model includes 5 dimensions: tangibles (physical facilities and the appearance of personnel), reliability (ability to perform the promised service dependably and accurately), responsiveness (willingness to help customers and provide prompt service), assurance (employee knowledge base which induces customer trust and confidence) and empathy (caring and individualized attention provided to customers by the service providers). The adaptability of dimensions of SERVQUAL makes it is widely used in many industries (banking, health care etc.). However, there are some researchers (Teas et al., 1992; Brady et al., 2002) who have raised concerns as to its validity, as well as definitional concerns related to the construct of expectations (Ueltschy, 2007). Cronin and Taylor developed a SERVPERF model also to measure service quality. They found expectations have no direct impact on customer satisfaction. Martensen et al. (2000) in a survey conducted in Denmark, also found that expectations have no or only a minimal impact on customer satisfaction and loyalty, especially for the telecommunication industry of Denmark. He thinks the value of "expectations" only exist on the theoretical level.

(c) In this new model, we are adding the "switching cost" as an important factor of customer loyalty. Based on the previous researches, switching cost has a significant impact on customer loyalty and it affects the relationship between customer satisfaction and customer loyalty.

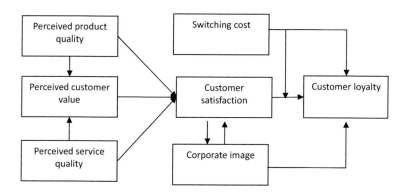

Figure 2.3: The New Model

As depicted above, the model explains that customer loyalty is affected by customer satisfaction, corporate image, and switching cost. Customer satisfaction comes from three aspects: perceived product quality, perceived service quality and perceived customer value. Switching cost not only can affect customer loyalty directly but also has influence on the relationship between customer satisfaction and customer loyalty.

Corporate image and customer satisfaction have mutual impact on each other.

Based on our model, we embody every factor into several concrete forms especially for mobile telecom sector in Nigeria and select eleven of them to test if these sub-factors really have connection with customer loyalty and which of them are more important in the mobile sector. Coverage of the area, call quality, SMS quality, and network quality are concrete forms for perceived product quality; convenient and reliable inquiring balance system and the service quality of service center and hotline are for perceived service quality, rating price of given quality is for perceived customer value; score accumulation and bonus and worry of troubles after change cell phone number are for switching cost; last but not least, advertisements of corporate image and corporate social responsibility are for corporate image. We suppose that these eleven concrete forms of factors have important influence on customer loyalty in Nigeria mobile communication industry.

CHAPTER THREE

3.1   Study Area

The target population in this work is the customers of mobile telephone users in Nigeria. However the area under study comprises of sampled respondents randomly selected from University of Ilorin, Ilorin. The mobile telephone service providers are also limited to four (4) of the GSM operators only for reasons earlier stated.

3.2   Method of Investigation

Research methodology defines the systematic and scientific procedures used to arrive at the results and findings for a study against which claims for knowledge are evaluated (Nachamias et al., 1996; Saunders et al., 2007). A methodology is therefore shaped by the perspectives the researcher chooses to approach a study.

Verhonic and Seaman (1998) as sited in Aina (2001) described research design as "a plan of study providing the overall framework for collecting data". This study will use sample *survey design* through a carefully selected sample to study a population of mobile telecom customers to understand variables likely to influence their loyalty towards their service provider. The research will be *descriptive* thereby schematically describing the characteristics of the population and *inferential* as inferences will be made from the samples examined to the population.

The respondents cut across all service providers in the GSM band available within the campus of Obafemi Awolowo University, Ile-Ife. Data was collected using copies of the questionnaire which was self administered.

3.3   Sampling Procedures

A sample size of four hundred (400) respondents will be selected based on researchers' judgment because of cost and time constraints. Using a larger sample in this survey would require large financial resources which we won't be able to afford. Again, the time limit within which the research is to be completed would not permit the use of larger sample size.

In selecting the sample of four hundred (400) respondents, a stratified simple random sampling will be used. This technique was chosen because the population consists of mobile networks in Nigeria, each being a stratum. This will be done by first identifying each of the mobile telecom networks within the target population as a stratum. Secondly, the total sample will be divided for each stratum according to the percentage of each stratum of mobile network in the entire industry. In selecting the percentages, we were guided by the available statistics of 2010 subscribers for each network (www.ncc.gov.ng, April 2010)

Finally, a simple random method will be used to select respondents for each of the mobile networks.

On the sample size for a survey research, Aina (2001) opined that:

> "Most books give formulae for calculating the sample size needed in order to achieve a certain level of accuracy or precision in estimating a characteristic of the population. However, it is not practicable to use these formulae because it is rare for any survey research to be confined to a single purpose; nearly always, it seek information on number of different variables (or attributes) and a sample that is quite big for one variable might be inadequate for another that requires greater precision."

It is in the light of this that the sample size for this study will be taken as an arbitrary number of 400 hundred (400) which the researcher believes should be adequate enough to gather the required data for the study apart from the reasons stated earlier.

The number of respondents per service provider will be selected based on the following formulae:

$$\frac{\text{Number of subscribers of a service provider}}{\text{Total Number of mobile phone subscribers}} \quad X \quad 400$$

The selection for his part of the sample is guided by the December 2009 data made available by the NCC. This is because the current data (April, 2010) does not reflect the break down of each provider's subscribers base. The sample size derived using the formulae above is as represented in **Table 3.1**

Table 3.1 Service Providers, their Subscriber Base and Selected Sample

S/N	SERVICE PROVIDER	SUBSCRIBERS	SELECTED SAMPLE
1	MTN	28,740,000	186
2	Globacom	16,228,556	105
3	Zain	14,935,770	97
4	Etisalat	1,835,870	12
	TOTALS	**61,998,716**	**400**

DATA SOURCE: NCC, 2009 (www.ncc.gov.ng)

3.4 Measurement of Variables

Variables under this study are made up of *categorical* data which form part of the question under the demographic variables and these include: age and service providers. These variables are also *nominal*. The first part of section B of the questionnaire consists of variable of the *ordinal* format and conforms to the 5-point Likert scale format measured by "strongly agree", "agree" "undecided" and "disagree", to "strongly disagree". The second part however has nominal data type. The first part of section C of the questionnaire also consists of variable of the *ordinal* format and conforms to the 5-point Likert scale format measured by "Very Satisfied", "Satisfied", "undecided", and "Unsatisfied" to "Very Unsatisfied" with the last question on the questionnaire been a *nominal* data type.

Frequency count, measures of central tendencies and dispersion was employed in the analysis of the variables. The weighted Average was also employed. A weighted average of the responses of the subjects used for this study was computed to capture the direction of their collective responses put together. In doing this, a weight was attached to each class of the responses and the number of respondents in each class is multiplied by the weight. The total of all this for a variable is then divided by the number of respondents, the ensuing value is then known as the weighted average of the response for that class. For example, the weighted average for response to Quality of phone call can be computed as this:

$(175*1) + (144*2) + (27*3) + (27*4) + (0*5) = 1536$

$WA = 552/348$

$= 1.6$

Since this value is closer to 2 which is the weight attached to "Agree" then we can say the direction of the collective response of the respondents is tending towards "Agreed"

3.5 Research Instrument

The instrument to be employed for the purpose of data collection in this study is the questionnaire. It comprises of closed and open ended questions. Efforts were however made to ensure that the questionnaire used was more of close-ended questions one so as to facilitate effective data analysis. The questionnaire has in all a total of twenty eight (4+12+13) questions in line with the research purpose. The questionnaire is a thematic one divided into three sections and described as follows:

SECTION A: DEMOGRAPHIC INFORMATION: The first part is the background information of interviewers. It consists by three questions. One is the *gender*: female or male; *age* and how many years the respondent have been a subscriber of the mobile phone service provider. The descriptors ranged from "less than one year", "1-2 years", "2-3 years", and "3-4 year", "4-5 years" to "more than 5 years".

SECTION B: CUSTOMER LOYALTY VARIABLES: The second part is testing which factors have an important impact on customer loyalty in the Nigeria telecom industry. These factors are considered from 3 parts: customer satisfaction (perceived quality, customer value), switching cost and corporate image. These are the perspectives this researcher after a thorough review of literature wants to consider as affecting a customers loyalty in the telecom industry. The questions are based on a five-point scale. The descriptors ranged from "strongly agree", "agree" "undecided" and "disagree", to "strongly disagree".

SECTION C: PROVIDER PERFORMANCE ON LOYALTY VARIABLES: The third part is to see the performance of the mobile telecom providers on these factors. This part aims to find out on which part (factor) the mobile telecom providers are performing well and which factors need to be improved upon. These questions are based on a five-point scale. The descriptors ranged from "Very Satisfied", "Satisfied", "undecided", and "Unsatisfied" to "Very Unsatisfied".

3.6   Validation of Research Instrument and Testing

In order to ensure the adequacy and reliability of the data collection instrument for the study, a face validity of the questionnaire was carried out by submitting a copy of the instrument to the study supervisor. The instrument was revised to ensure clarity, appropriateness of language and expression to the respondents. To ensure internal validity, an intensive literature review was carried out, so the eleven sub-factors were generated from the exercise and they are all related to customer loyalty at least from former researchers' opinions.

Reliability is the consistency of a measurement. Our questionnaires was tested among some few students at the early phase, base on the feedback, we re-organized it time by time before arriving at the final version of questionnaire which was easily to be

44

understood and answered; to make sure most of the respondents our questions with less effort.

Aina, (2001) posited that a data collection instrument can only be deemed valid if it measures the quality desired truly and accurately. To achieve this, a good instrument with "high validity and reliability is required, hence the reason for planning to carry out the reliability test on the research instrument for this survey. Reliability is concerned with the consistency with which an instrument measures the variables it is supposed to measure which implies the instruments ability to return same result when procedures such as data collection are repeated. Validity is concerned with whether the findings are really what they appear to be and hence related to ensuring that the instrument actually measures the phenomenon that it is supposed to measure.

Table 3.2: Measurement Scale Properties

Measure	Number of Items	Reliability (Cronbach's Alpha)
Customer Loyalty	11	.712
Provider Performance	12	.868

3.7   Method of Data Analysis

Data generated from this work was analyzed descriptively using simple frequency count and measures of central tendency, to describe the general distribution and trends in the data. Inferences were based on the use of weighted average methods were also used to examine relationships between variables. Statistical investigation was also carried out to determine the relationship that exists between some demographic variables and the customer loyalty variables. Most of the analysis was carried out using Statistical Package for Social Sciences (SPSS) Version 11 and Microsoft Excel 2007.

CHAPTER FOUR

4.1 Response Rate

Four Hundred (400) copies of the questionnaire were given out to respondent. The percentage retrieved in total amounted to 87% accounting for 348 copies of the questionnaire administered. All of the respondents in this survey were students of University of Ilorin, North Central Nigeria. In distribution, 55% representing 220 of the questionnaire were given to female students in different levels of study and the remaining 45% representing 180 were given to their male counterparts also in different levels of study.

The rationale behind giving more numbers to the female students stems from the fact that anecdotal evidence suggest that females spend more time on the phone than males.

4.2 Respondents' Characteristics and Classification

Female respondents had a 94.5% response rate (208 of 220) while the male respondents returned 77.8% (140 of 180) as shown in figure 4.1. The two sexes put together yields a response rate as depicted in figure 4.1 below.

Table 4.1: Retrieval Rate by Gender

Gender	Distributed	%	Retrieved	%
Male	180	45	140	77.8
Female	220	55	208	94.5
Total	**400**	**100**	**348**	

(Source: Field Survey 2010)

Figure 4.1: Respondents' distribution by Gender

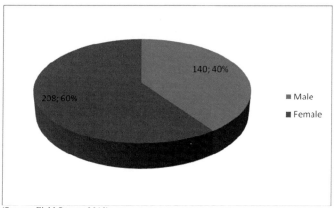

(Source: Field Survey 2010)

The dominant age group of the respondents falls in the range between 21 – 25 years and this account for more than half of the respondents. Very few of the respondents fall in the 31-35 and above 35 years age range with the two categories accounting for only 2.8% of the respondents. The full distribution of respondents by their age group is presented below

Table 4.2: Distribution of respondents by Age

Age Group	N	%
16-20	99	28.4
21-25	178	51.1
26-30	61	17.5
31-35	6	1.7
Above 35	4	1.1
Total	**348**	**100.0**

(Source: Field Survey 2010)

Subscribers of MTN (N=161) as shown by **figure 4.2** below form the bulk of the respondents as a single provider. However the other three key players in the industry (Glo N=91, Zain N=85 and Etisalat N=11) account for more than 50% of the respondents.

Figure 4.2: Distribution of Respondents by Mobile Phone Network Provider

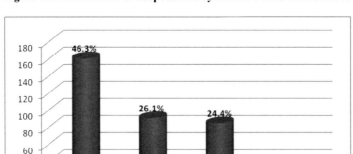

(Source: Field Survey 2010)

More than half (66.1%) of the respondents have been using their mobile phone providers for 5 years and above and almost 34% represents the pool of respondents that have been with their service provider for less than a year to 4 years. The table below refers.

Table 4.3: Distribution of Respondents by Duration with Preferred Mobile Network Provider

Duration(years)	N	%
<1 year	10	2.9
1 - 2	16	4.6
3 – 4	92	26.4
5 and above	230	66.1
Total	**348**	**100.0**

(Source: Field Survey 2010)

4.3   Presentation and Analysis of Data According to Research Objectives

4.3.1   Factors that specifically affect the loyalty of mobile telecom users.

The opinions of the respondents concerning the listed variables as influencing their loyalty towards their mobile service provider is highlighted below (Table 4.4), were such that more than half of them agreed that the *Quality of Phone Call* (319, 91.7%), *Network Coverage Area* (315, 90.5%), *Quality of SMS* (208, 59.8), *Mobile Internet* (248, 60.3%), *Customers Service Call* (275, 79.1%), *Given Quality Price Rating* (280, 80.5%), *Bonus and free Service* (283, 91.3%), *Changing cell phone number* (307, 88.2%), (151, 69.6%), (154, 71.0%), *Social Responsibility* (302, 86.8%) are variables capable of influencing their loyalty. However, for *Service Centre Quality* (129, 36%) and *Brand Image (Adverts)*, (104, 29.9%) far less than 40% agreed to these two factors as being capable of influencing their loyalty towards their service providers.

Table 4.4: Factors Influencing Customer Loyalty

	RESPONSES									
	Strongly Agreed		Agreed		Undecided		Disagree		Strongly Disagree	
Loyalty Influencing Variables	N	%	N	%	N	%	N	%	N	%
Quality of Phone Call	175	50.3	144	41.4	27	7.8	2	0.6	-	-
Network Coverage Area	136	39.1	179	51.4	30	8.6	2	0.6	1	0.3
Quality of SMS	78	22.4	130	37.4	61	17.5	68	19.5	11	3.2
Mobile Internet	97	27.9	151	43.4	70	20.1	24	6.9	6	1.7
Service Centre Quality	21	6.0	108	31.0	107	30.7	98	28.2	14	4.0
Customers Service Call	105	30.2	170	48.9	55	15.8	16	4.6	2	0.6
Given Quality Price Rating	126	36.2	154	44.3	53	15.2	15	4.3	-	-
Bonus and free Service	124	35.6	159	45.7	56.1	16	9	2.6	-	-
Troubles of changing cell phone number	123	35.3	184	52.9	37	10.6	3	0.9	1	0.3
Brand Image (Adverts)	9	2.6	95	27.3	115	33.0	110	31.6	19	5.5
Social Responsibility	146	42.0	156	44.8	37	10.6	8	2.3	1	0.3

(Source: Field Survey 2010)

Table 4.5: Weighted Average of Responses to Factors Influencing Loyalty N=348

S/N	Loyalty Variables	(1) SA	(2) A	(3) U	(4) D	(5) SD	TOTAL	WA	REM
1.	Quality of Phone Call	175	144	27	2	0	552	1.6	A
2.	Network Coverage Area	136	179	30	2	1	597	1.7	A
3.	Quality of SMS	78	130	61	68	11	848	2.4	A
4.	Mobile Internet	97	151	70	24	6	735	2.1	A
5.	Service Centre Quality	21	108	107	98	14	1020	2.9	U
6.	Customers Service Call	105	170	55	16	2	684	2.0	A
7.	Given Quality Price Rating	126	154	53	15	0	653	1.9	A
8.	Bonus and free Service	124	159	56	9	0	646	1.9	A
9.	Troubles of changing cell phone number	123	184	37	3	1	619	1.8	A
10.	Brand Image (Adverts)	9	95	115	110	19	1079	3.1	U
11.	Social Responsibility	146	156	37	8	1	606	1.7	A

(Source: Field Survey 2010)
Key: SA= Strongly Agreed, A=Agreed, U=Undecided, D=Disagree, SD=Strongly Disagree, WA=Weighted Average, REM=Remarks

Therefore from Tables 4.4 and 4.5 above, we can deduce that the respondents agreed that all the eleven variables with the exception of Service Centre Quality and Brad Image are capable of Influencing their loyalty towards their mobile phone service. Their response on these two variables might not be unconnected with the fact that customers rarely visit service centers and might not really know how this might affect their loyalty. Brand Image on the other hand is always seen as particular to the service provider and does little to add value to the consumer.

Table 4.6: Indexes of Measures of Central Tendencies and Measures of Dispersion of Loyalty Variables

Loyalty Variables	Mean	Median	Mode	Std. Dev	Range	Min	Max
Quality of Phone Call	1.59	1.00	1	.658	3	1	4
Network Coverage Area	1.72	2.00	2	.668	4	1	5
Quality of SMS	2.44	2.00	2	1.131	4	1	5
Mobile Internet	2.11	2.00	2	.949	4	1	5
Service Centre Quality	1.97	2.00	2	.834	4	1	5
Customers Service Call	2.93	3.00	2	.996	4	1	5
Given Quality Price Rating	1.88	2.00	2	.821	3	1	4
Bonus and free Service	1.86	2.00	2	.776	3	1	4
Troubles of changing cell phone number	1.78	2.00	2	.687	4	1	5
Brand Image (Adverts)	3.10	3.00	3	.950	4	1	5
Social Responsibility	1.7	2.00	2	.76	4	1	5

(Source: Field Survey 2010)

We used mean to evaluate the influence of every variable and then decide whether the variable should be accepted or not. We set 1 to represent very important and 5 to represent not important (as coded in SPSS). So if the mean is close to 1 it implies most of the respondents think the factor plays an important role and therefore capable of in influencing their loyalty towards their service provider. On the other way round, if the mean is close to 1, it means most of interviewees think the factor does not play an important role in determining their loyalty towards their service provider. In this thesis we set Strongly Agree =1, Agree = 2; Undecided=3; Disagree=4; Strongly Disagree=5. So from the table presented above (Table 4.6), our respondents tend towards agreeing with most of the eleven listed variables as capable of influencing their loyalty towards their service provider with means ranging from 1.7 to 2.4. It should however be noted that customer service call and brand image fall in the "undecided zone".

Median is the average of the central pair and is calculated by arranging all the observations from lowest to highest and then picking the middle one or calculating the average of the central pair. Medians of all the listed variables are 2 with the exception of

51

Quality of phone call which has 1. Also customer service call and brand image has a median of 3.

Mode is the value that occurs most frequently. As shown in table 4.6 above and similar to the median, the modal values of the loyalty influencing variables are 1 with the exception of Service Center Quality and Brand Image Advert that measured 2. This implies that majority of he respondents are of the opinion that these factors are important influencing factors in customer loyalty.

Standard deviation is a measure of the dispersion of values. A low Standard deviation means the data points tend to be very close to the mean, and high Std. deviation indicates the data are "spread out" over a large range of values. All the Standard deviations of the customer loyalty variables are less than 1 with the exception of SMS Quality which has a Standard deviation of 1.13. This means the data in every series are very close to their means. Quality of Phone Call provided by the service providers are closest to its mean 1.59 with a Standard Deviation of 0.658 and Quality of SMS data are the most dispersed among the variables with a Standard Deviation of 1.13 to its mean of 2.44 (Table 4.6).

Range is calculated by subtracting minimum value from maximum value of the given data. It represents the length of the observation. Quality of Phone Call, Given Quality Price Rating, Bonus and free Service has a Range of 3 and a maximum value of 4.This indicates that on these variables respondents only chose between "strongly agree" and "Disagree" and no respondent chose "Strongly Disagree". Others have a range of 4 with a maximum value of 5 meaning respondents selected all the 5 available options on the rest variables.

4.3.2 Influence of Gender, Age and Mobile Phone use Duration on Loyalty Variables

We also want to determine if the duration of use of mobile phones, age and gender of the respondents might have significant effect on their responses thereby affecting the outcome of the research.

Table 4.7 below shows the means of responses to loyalty variables in terms of age. The data was selected using the sort cases command of SPSS. Through this each data set as it regards the different age categories were selected separately. Through this, the independent mean of the data set was calculated and the result is as presented below.

Table 4.7: Influence of Age on Loyalty Variables

S/N	Loyalty Variables	16-20	21-25	26-30	31-35	Above 35
1.	Quality of Phone Call	1.7	1.6	1.5	1.5	1.8
2.	Network Coverage Area	1.7	1.7	1.8	2.0	1.5
3.	Quality of SMS	2.7	2.4	2.2	2.2	2.0
4.	Mobile Internet	2.0	2.1	2.4	2.0	1.5
5.	Service Centre Quality	1.8	2.0	2.2	1.8	1.5
6.	Customers Service Call	2.8	3.0	3.0	3.0	2.8
7.	Given Quality Price Rating	1.8	1.9	1.9	2.0	1.3
8.	Bonus and free Service	1.9	1.8	1.8	2.0	2.0
9.	Changing Cell Phone Numbers	1.7	1.8	1.8	2.0	2.5
10.	Brand Image (Adverts)	3.1	3.3	2.7	3.0	2.3
11.	Social Responsibility	1.7	1.7	2.0	2.0	2.3
	Total	22.9	23.3	23.3	23.5	21.5
	Average	2.08	2.19	2.19	2.14	1.95

(Source: Field Survey 2010)

The results shows that difference in age results into no significant difference in the responses of the respondents as the average value for each age category falls around 2 and his is also the same with the mean value of data sets put together

The same (sort cases) was used for gender and duration of mobile phone use as it relates to respondents responses to loyalty variables. Table 4.8 presents the result of the case analysis

Table 4.8: Influence of Gender and Mobile Phone use Duration on Loyalty Variables

S/N	Loyalty Variables	Gender		Phone Use Duration (Years)			
		Male	Female	<1	1-2	3-4	5&above
1.	Quality of Phone Call	1.6	1.6	1.6	1.4	1.6	1.6
2.	Network Coverage Area	1.7	1.7	1.8	1.6	1.7	1.7
3.	Quality of SMS	2.5	2.4	2.8	2.2	2.6	2.4
4.	Mobile Internet	2.1	2.1	2.3	2.0	2.1	2.1
5.	Service Centre Quality	1.9	2.0	1.9	2.9	3.1	2.9
6.	Customers Service Call	2.8	3.0	2.3	1.8	2.1	2.0
7.	Given Quality Price Rating	1.9	1.9	2.5	2.1	1.9	1.8
8.	Bonus and free Service	1.9	1.8	1.7	1.6	1.9	1.9
9.	Changing Cell Phone Numbers	1.9	1.7	1.7	1.6	1.8	1.8
10.	Brand Image (Adverts)	3.1	3.1	3.1	3.5	3.0	3.1
11.	Social Responsibility	1.8	1.7	1.8	1.8	1.6	1.8
	Total	23.2	23.0	23.5	22.5	23.4	23.1
	Average	2.10	2.09	2.13	2.05	2.13	2.09

(Source: Field Survey 2010)

The results also shows that difference in gender and the duration of mobile phone use results into no significant difference in the responses of the respondents as the average value for each age category falls around 2 and his is also the same with the mean value of data sets put together

4.3.3 Performance of the telecom service providers against the identified factors.

The opinions of the respondents concerning the performance of their service providers on the listed variables potentially capable of influencing their loyalty towards their mobile service provider are highlighted below (Table 4.9). Their opinion were such that far less than half of the respondents agreed that the service providers have been able to

54

perform satisfactorily in terms of *Quality of Phone Call* (73, 20.9%), *Mobile Internet* (82, 25.6%), *Customers Service Call* (63, 18.1%), *Given Quality Price Rating* (58, 16.7%), *Bonus and free Service* (141, 40.5%), *Social Responsibility* (55, 15.8%), *General Satisfaction* (47, 13.5%). For *Service Centre Quality* (170, 48.9%) was recorded.

However, respondents were satisfied with the performance of their service provider in terms of *Network Coverage Area* (265, 75.3%) while the rest are either undecided or not satisfied. This might just be evidenced by the fact that mobile phone service providers in Nigeria are vigorously pursuing expansion strategies to cover the nook and crannies of the nation. In the same vain, respondents were also satisfied with the *Quality of SMS* (275, 79.02%) and *Brand Image* (Adverts) as the variable also received a more than 70% responses indicating the satisfaction of he respondents towards the variable.

Table 4.9: Service providers Performance Table

	RESPONSES									
	Very Satisfied		Satisfied		Undecided		Unsatisfied		Very Unsatisfied	
Loyalty Influencing Variables	N	%	N	%	N	%	N	%	N	%
Quality of Phone Call	3	0.9	70	20.1	113	22.5	137	39.4	25	7.2
Network Coverage Area	67	19.3	195	56.0	58	16.7	23	6.6	5	1.4
Quality of SMS	27	7.8	248	71.3	48	13.8	12	3.4	13	3.7
Mobile Internet	5	1.4	77	22.1	108	31.0	136	39.1	22	6.3
Service Centre Quality	33	9.5	137	39.4	51	14.7	103	29.6	24	6.9
Customers Service Call	7	2.0	56	16.1	101	29.0	141	40.5	43	12.4
Given Quality Price Rating	13	3.7	45	12.9	81	23.3	162	46.6	47	13.5
Bonus and free Service	40	11.5	101	29.0	85	24.4	96	27.6	26	7.5
Brand Image (Adverts)	24	6.9	251	72.1	42	12.1	14	4.0	17	4.9
Social Responsibility	10	2.9	45	12.9	85	24.4	137	39.4	71	20.4
General Satisfaction	4	1.1	43	12.4	75	21.6	166	47.7	60	17.2

(Source: Field Survey 2010)

Similar to what was done to the loyalty variables; a weighted average was also computed for the responses on the performance of the service providers on loyalty variables. The summary of the findings is represented in Table 4.10 below:

Table 4.10: Weighted Average of Responses to Performance on Loyalty Variables
N=348

S/N	Loyalty Variables	(1) VS	(2) S	(3) U	(4) US	(5) VU	Total	WA	REM
1.	Quality of Phone Call	3	70	113	137	25	1655	4.8	VU
2.	Network Coverage Area	67	195	58	23	5	748	2.1	S
3.	Quality of SMS	27	248	48	12	13	780	2.2	S
4.	Mobile Internet	5	77	108	136	22	1137	3.3	U
5.	Service Centre Quality	33	137	51	103	24	992	2.9	U
6.	Customers Service Call	7	56	101	141	43	1701	4.9	VU
7.	Given Quality Price Rating	13	45	81	162	47	1229	3.5	US
8.	Bonus and free Service	40	101	85	96	26	1011	2.9	U
9.	Brand Image (Adverts)	24	251	42	14	17	793	2.2	S
10.	Social Responsibility	10	45	85	137	71	1258	3.6	US
11.	General Satisfaction	4	43	75	166	60	1279	3.7	US

(Source: Field Survey 2010)

Key: VS=Very Satisfied, S=Satisfied, U=Undecided, US= Unsatisfied, VU=Very Unsatisfied

The respondents based on the above data tend towards been very unsatisfied on the variables: Quality of Phone Call and Customer Service Call. The data shows they were undecided on the performance of the service providers on Mobile Internet, Service Centre Quality and Bonus & Free Service. However they were satisfied on Network Coverage Area, Quality of SMS and Brand Image. Also, they were unsatisfied on Given Quality Price Rating, Social Responsibility as well as on General Satisfaction. Even though respondents were undecided on some variables the fact that they are not generally satisfied could mean that the variable with undecided response might be because those variables are less used by the respondents. For example very few people will have a reason to go to the customer service centers and so also those people with internet service on their phones probably because of its cost.

Table 4.11: Indexes of Measures of Central Tendencies and Measures of Dispersion of Performance on Loyalty Variables

	Mean	Median	Mode	Std. Dev	Range	Min	Max
Quality of Phone Call	3.32	3.00	4	.904	4	1	5
Network Coverage Area	2.15	2.00	2	.856	4	1	5
Quality of SMS	2.24	2.00	2	.796	4	1	5
Mobile Internet	3.27	3.00	4	.924	4	1	5
Service Centre Quality	2.85	3.00	2	1.152	4	1	5
Customers Service Call	3.45	4.00	4	.970	4	1	5
Given Quality Price Rating	3.53	4.00	4	1.002	4	1	5
Bonus and free Service	2.91	3.00	2	1.149	4	1	5
Brand Image (Adverts)	2.28	2.00	2	.845	4	1	5
Social Responsibility	3.61	4.00	4	1.039	4	1	5
General Satisfaction	3.68	4.00	4	.940	4	1	5

(Source: Field Survey 2010)

From the table presented above (Table 4.8), and using the mean based on previous explanation of its application, our respondents were mostly undecided on the status of the variables: *Quality of Phone Call, Mobile Internet, Bonus/free Service, Service Centre Quality and Customers Service Call* as the means of these variable range between 2.85 and 3.45. *Network Coverage Area, Quality of SMS, and Brand Image (Adverts)* appeared satisfactorily disposed to as their means range from 2.15 to 2.28. It is however noted that *Given Quality Price, Rating Social Responsibility and General Satisfaction* all have a mean of more than 3.5 and hence can be interpreted as been unsatisfactorily disposed to.

The medians of all the listed variables fall between 2 and 4. The variables whose medians are 2 tend to have a mean close to 2 and invariably are the variables that respondents were satisfied with in terms of performance of the service providers. Other variables with median of above 2 returned a median value close to 3 and 4. As shown in Table 4.11 above, the modal values of the loyalty variables in this case are either 2 or 4. This implies that majority of the respondents selected "Satisfied" and "Unsatisfied".

The range of the all the variables here is 5, showing that the length of the observation here covers all the variables with the implication that respondents selected all the 5 available options for al the variables.

4.3.4   How service providers can better enhance the loyalty of their customers.

To address the third research objective which has to do with how service providers can enhance the loyalty of their customers, respondents were asked to select the variables they consider as key factors likely to impact more on their loyalty towards their service provider. Their responses are captured below in Figure 4.3 as follows:

Figure 4.3: Responses on Most Important Loyalty Variables

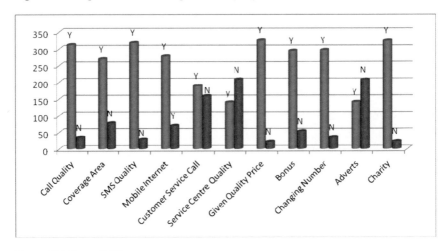

(Source: Field Survey 2010)

More than 75% of the respondents agreed that the variables: Call Quality. Coverage Area, SMS Quality, Mobile Internet, Given Quality Price Bonus & Free Service, Changing Mobile Number and Social Responsibility are the most important in deciding/influencing their loyalty towards their service provider. On the other way round, more than 60% of the respondents consider Adverts and Service Centre Quality as not too important in deciding their loyalty. Though more respondents believe Customer Service Call is also very important but the difference between the respondents considering the variable as very important and those considering it otherwise is a little narrow.

To this extent, the first eight variables mentioned above which the respondents considered as very important have a very strong influencing factor in enhancing the loyalty of customers. Therefore to enhance the loyalty of customers, these variables will require a critical review by the service providers with the aim of improving upon them.

Respondents were also asked if they will recommend their present service provider to their family and friends. More than half (199, 57.2%) says they will recommend their service provider to their family and friends while the rest says no.

Figure 4.4: Recommendation of Service Provider

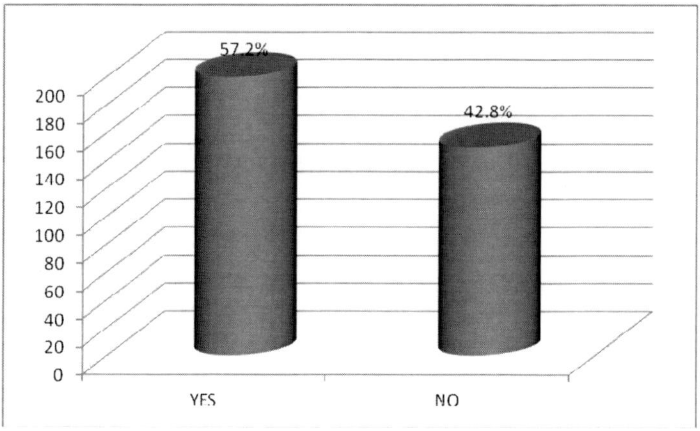

(Source: Field Survey 2010)

This response despite not been generally satisfied with the services provided can be linked to the fact that consumers will have to make do with a product or service as long as there is no viable alternative to ameliorate the deficiencies in the current one they are using. Then with relatives been on the same network they tend to benefit in terms lower tariff of intra network transactions.

CHAPTER FIVE

5.1   Summary

The concept of customer loyalty is important in almost every industry and appears much more important in Mobile telecommunication because of it low switching cost and therefore calls for continual research. This is much more important because the industry in Nigeria is still at its infancy at least when compared to the advanced economies and so there is a need to very well understand the dimensions capable of influencing customer loyalty in order to adequately prepare for the challenges ahead and to ensure that an appropriate foundation is laid to achieve customer loyalty.

The purpose of this study was to investigate what factors have important influence on customer loyalty in the Nigerian Mobile Telecommunication industry as well as the performance of selected service providers on the factors. The study was carried on from the perspective of the subscribers (users) to gain a general understanding of what they (users) will want in order to be loyal to their service providers. Eleven factors were selected through a careful literature review of previous researches on customer loyalty to study their importance on Nigeria's Mobile Telecommunication Industry customer loyalty. We also investigated how mobile telecom operators in Nigeria can better enhance the loyalty of their customers, and then gave a general recommendation to the operators in order to increase their customer's loyalty.

5.2   Conclusion

Knowledge generated from user perspective studies is capable of helping firms in the development of veritable solutions towards ensuring that the consumer/customer side of the issue of discuss is well understood and taken care of. Ensuring loyalty of customers is a lifeline for the continued existence of the service providers and so there is the need for service providers to ensure the loyalty of their subscribers. In this study, we contribute to the need to evolve strategies that can ensure the effectiveness and efficiency of Mobile Phone Service providers to reposition them in the highly competitive industry.

According to our study, quality of phone call, network coverage, SMS quality, mobile internet, customer service call, given quality price rating, bonus and free service, troubles of changing cell phone number and corporate social responsibility have important influence on customer loyalty in Nigeria Mobile Telecom sector (Table 4.5) while subscribers don't seem to see service centre quality and brand image as capable of influencing their decision to be loyal to their service provider or not. We also found out that age, gender and the duration of use (Tables 4.7 and 4.8) has no impact on the responses of the respondents; implying that the three variables (age, gender and duration of use) has no significant influence on loyalty variables.

While the above listed variables are generally considered for loyalty variables, Call Quality, Coverage Area, SMS Quality, Mobile Internet, Given Quality Price Bonus & Free Service, Changing Mobile Number and Social Responsibility (Figure 4.3) constitute the highly rated variables and the most important in deciding/influencing their loyalty towards their service provider. Though important, Customer Service Call was not seen as important as the above listed variable. However, Adverts and Service Centre Quality were described as not too important in deciding their loyalty.

To this extent, the first eight variables mentioned above which the respondents considered as very important have a very strong influencing factor in enhancing the loyalty of customers. Therefore to enhance the loyalty of customers, these variables will require a critical review by the service providers with the aim of improving upon them. While it was discovered that a lot of the respondents are satisfied with the corporate image advert of the firms same factor was not deemed important to influence loyalty.

Comparing the loyalty variables in the Nigerian environment to the other countries reviewed in this study, similarities exists in areas like call quality, coverage area, mobile internet and rating price of given quality. However, SMS quality, troubles after changing numbers and social responsibility is peculiar to our study. The first might probably be largely due to its low cost and prevalence among students while the later emanates from fact that Nigeria is yet to adopt Mobile Number Portability (MNP) which ensures that a subscriber can migrate to another service provider but still retain his/her old number. To this extent, the retention of customers that the service providers are enjoying now could be largely attributable to lack of MNP, presenting a "false loyalty" atmosphere. Therefore providers should enhance their service delivery so that when MNP comes in force, they will not end up loosing their customers. While it was discovered that a lot of the respondents are satisfied with the corporate image advert of the firms same factor was not deemed important to influence loyalty.

6.2   Recommendation

The service providers should keep their good performance as observed in areas like coverage area and brand image. They should however embark on drives that will reduce to its barest minimum drop calls, improve call quality and SMS delivery which is likely to make subscribers perceive given quality as high. These can be achieved by employing improved technology and increased investment. Efforts should also be geared towards improving upon corporate social responsibility and bonuses given to subscribers. They should not only be sponsors of recreational and sports activities but be an active participant in charity events to establish a good corporate image. So also, they should not only advertise their product but also advertise themselves and should add corporate culture into these kind of commercials.

BIBLIOGRAPHY

ACSI: Fornell, C. Johnson, M. D., 1996. The American customer satisfaction index: Nature, purpose and findings, *Journal of Marketing*, 60. 7-19

Ahn, J. H., Han, S. P., Lee Y. S., 2006. Customer churn analysis: Churn determinants and mediation effects of partial defection in the Korean mobile telecommunications service industry, *Telecommunications Policy*, 30, 552-569.

Amine, A., 1998. Consumers' true brand loyalty: the central role of commitment, *Journal of Strategic Marketing*. 6. 305-319

Anderson, E. W. Sullivan, M. W. 1993. The antecedent and consequences of customer satisfaction for firms. *Marketing Science*, 12. 125-144.

Andreasen, A. Drumwright, M. 2001. In: Andreasen, A. (Ed.), *Alliances and Ethics in SocialMarketing in Ethical Issues in Social Marketing*. Washington, DC: Georgetown University Press,

Andres K. 2007, Affecting customer loyalty: do different factors have various influences in different loyalty levels?, *University of Tartu - Faculty of Economics & Business Administration Working Paper Series*. 58. 3-30.

Aydin, S. Ozer, G. Arasil, O. 2005, Customer loyalty and the effect of switching costs as a moderator variable: A case in the Turkish mobile phone market. *Marketing Intelligence & Planningl*. 23. 89-103.

Bandyopadhyay, S. Martell, M. 2007. Does attitudinal loyalty influence behavioral loyalty. *Journal of Retailing & Consumer Services*. 14. 35-45.

Barich, H. Kotler, P. 1991, A framework for marketing image management, *Sloan Management Review*. 32.94-104.

Bitner, M. J. Hubbert, A. R. 1994. *Encounter Satisfaction versus Overall Satisfaction versus Quality, Service Quality New Directions in Theory and Practices*. London: Sage Publications. 72-95.

Blodgett, J.G. Hill, D.J. Tax, S.S. 1997, The effects of distributive, procedural, and interactional justice on post-complaint behavior, *Journal of Retailing*. 31. 185-210.

Bodet, G. 2008. Customer satisfaction and loyalty in service: Two concepts, four constructs, several relationships. *Journal of Retailing & Consumer Services*. 15. 156-163.

Brady, M.K. Cronin, J.J. Brand, R.R. 2002. Performance-only measurement of service quality: a replication and extension. *Journal of Business Research*. 55. 17-31.

Brown, T.J. Dacin, P.A. 1997. The company and the product: corporate associations and consumer product responses. *Journal of Marketing*, 6. 68–84.

Brunner T. A. Stöcklin, M. Opwis, K. 2008. Satisfaction, image and loyalty: new versus experienced customers. *European journal of marketing*. 42. 1095-1105.

Burnham, T. A., Frels, J. K., Mahajan, V., 2003. Consumer switching costs: a typology antecedents, and consequences, *Journal of the Academy of Marketing Science*, 31, 109-126.

Butcher, K. Sparks, B. O'Callaghan, F. 2001, Evaluative and relational influences on service loyalty. *International Journal of Service Industry Managemental*. 12. 310-328.

Capizzi, M. T. and Ferguson, R. (2005). Loyalty trends for the twenty-first century. *Journal of Consumer Marketing, 22*, 72-81.

Caruana, A. 2004. The impact of switching costs on customer loyalty: A study among corporate customers of mobile telephone. *Journal of Targeting, Measurement & Analysis for Marketing*. 12. 256-269.

Cary W. and Adams A. (2009). Customer satisfaction and customer loyalty are the best predictors of customer retention. *Online Journal*. Available from: http://www.adamssixsigma.com/Newsletters/customers_results.htm (accessed 5, May 2009)

Cassel, C. and Eklof, (2001). Modeling customer satisfaction and loyalty on aggregate levels: Experience from the ECSI pilot study. *Total Quality Management*, 12, 834-841.

Chaudhuri, A. and Holbrook, M. B. (2001). The Chain of Effects from Brand Trust and Brand Affect to Brand Performance: The Role of Brand Loyalty. *Journal of Marketing*. 65. 81-94.

Chen J. S. and Ching, R. (2006). The Study of Mobile Customer Relationship Management and Loyalty. *2006 International Conference on Service Systems and Service Management*. 1. 67-72

Chris, D. Anne, G. and Nigel, W. (1998). Barclays Life customer satisfaction and loyalty tracking survey: a demonstration of customer loyalty research in practice. *Journal of International Journal of Bank Marketing*. 16. 287 – 292.

Chwo-ming, Y., Lei-yu, W., Yu-ching, C., Hsing-shia, T., 2005. Perceived quality, customer satisfaction, and customer loyalty: the case of lexus in Taiwan. *Total quality management & business excellence*, 16, 707-719

Dick, A. S. Basu, K. 1994. Customer loyalty: toward an integrated conceptual framework. *Journal of the Academy of Marketing Science*. 22. 99-1 13.

Dodds, W. B. Monroe, K. B. Grewal, D. 1991. Effects of Price, Brand, and Store Information on Buyers' Product Evaluations. *Journal of Marketing Research.* 28. 307-320.

Dowling, G. R., Uncles, M., 1997. Do Customer Loyalty Programs Really Work? *Sloan Management Review*, 38, 71-83

Ehrenberg, A.S.C. Norman ,P. 1991. Repeat buying—facts, theory and applications. *The Statistician.* 40. 349-350.

Ehrenberg, Goodhardt G.J., 1997. Understanding Buyer Behavior. *New York: J. Walter Thompson and the Market Research Corporation of America.*

ECSI (1998): European Customer Satisfaction Index------Foundation and Structure for Harmonised National Pilot Projects. Report prepared by ECSI Technical Committee. *ECSI Document*, No. 005, 1 20- 11- 98.

Fadebiyi, I. (2009) Industry Analysis: Nigerian Mobile Telcom Available from: http: // www.prlog.org/10242511-industry-analysis-nigerian-mobile-telco.pdf [Accessed March 29, 2010].

Gerpott, T; Rams, W; Schindler, A, 2001. Customer retention, loyalty and satisfaction in the German mobile cellular telecommunications market. *Telecommunications Policy.* 25. 249–269.

Groholdt, L. Martensen, A. Kristensen, K. 2000. The relationship between customer satisfaction and loyalty: Cross-industry differences. *Total Quality Management.* 11. 509-514.

Hu, H. H. Kandampully J. Juwaheer T. D. 2009. Relationships and impacts of service quality, perceived value, customer satisfaction, and image: an empirical study. *Service Industries Journal.* 29. 111-126.

Jacoby, J. Chestnut, R. 1978. *Brand Loyalty: Measurement and Management.* New York: Wiley.

Jacoby, J. and Kyner, B. 1973. Brand loyalty versus repeat purchasing behaviour. *Journal of Marketing Research.* February. 1-9.

Jay K. 2007, Do hoteliers need to manage image to retain loyal customers. *International Journal of Contemporary Hospitality Management.* 19. 435-443.

Jennifer K., 2008. Is customer loyalty an outdated concept? *Journal of Consumer Marketing*

Jia, S. H. Yan., H. R. 2005. Empirical analysis on the forming model of customer loyalty: the case study of mobile communication service, Systems and Services Management, *2005 International Conference on.* 1, 133-137

Jones, M. A. Mothersbaugh, D. L. Betty, S. E. 2000. Switching barriers and repurchase intentions in services. *Journal of Retailing.* 76. 259–272.

Jones, M. A. Suh, J. 2000. Transaction-specific satisfaction and overall satisfaction: an empirical analysis. *Journal of Services Marketing.* 14. 147-160.

Jones, T.O. Sasser, W.E. 1995. Why satisfied customers defect. Harvard Business Review. 73. 88-102.

Kashyap, R. Bojanic, D. C. 2000. A structural analysis of value, quality, and price perceptions of business and leisure travelers. *Journal of Travel Research.* 39. 45-52.

Keller, K.1993. Conceptualizing, measuring, and managing customer based equity. Journal of Marketing. 57. 1-22.

Kim M. K., Park, M. C. Jeong, D. H. 2004. The effects of customer satisfaction and switching barrier on customer loyalty in Korean mobile telecommunication services. *Telecommunications Policy.* 2. 145-159.

Kim, Y. P. Lee, S. H. Yun, D. G. 2004. Integrating current and competitive service-qualitylevel analyses for service-quality improvement programs, *Managing Service Quality.* 14. 288-296.

Lee J. KimY. Lee, J.D. Park Y. 2006. Estimating the extent of potential competition in the Korean mobile telecommunications market: Switching costs and number portability. *International Journal of Industrial Organization,* 24, 107-124.

Lee, J. Feick, L. 2001. The impact of switching costs on the customer satisfaction-loyalty link: Mobile phone service in France. *Journal of Services Marketing.* 15. 35–48.

Li, L. 2008. Study of the Relationship between Customer Satisfaction and Loyalty in Telecom Enterprise. *4th International Conference on Wireless Communications, Networking and Mobile Computing,* 1-7.

Long, Y. L. and Jen, C. 2004. An Integrated Analysis of Relationship between Service Quality, Relationship Quality, Relationship Value and Customers' Loyalty-An Example of Consumers of Mobile Telecommunication Industry. *Tamsui Oxford Journal of Economics and Business.* 12. 73-112.

MacInnis, D.J. Price, L.L. 1987. The role of imagery in information processing: review and extensions. *Journal of Consumer Research.* 13. 473-91.

Martensen, A. Gronholdt, L. Kristensen, K. 2000, The drivers of customer satisfaction and loyalty: cross-industry findings from Denmark. *Total Quality Management.* 11. 544-553.

Monroe, K. B. 1990. *Pricing: Making Profitable Decisions*. New York: McGraw-Hill.

Muller, E., 1998. Customer loyalty programs. *Sloan Management Review*, 39, 4-6.

Nguyen, N. Leblanc, G. 2001, Corporate image and corporate reputation in customers' retention decisions in services. *Journal of Retailing and Consumer Services*. 8. 227-36.

Oh, H. Parks, C. S. 1997. Customer satisfaction and service quality: A critical review of the literature and research implications for the hospitality industry, *Hospitality Research Journal*. 20. 36-64.

Oh, H. 1999, Service quality, customer satisfaction, and customer value: A holistic perspective. *International Journal of Hospitality Management*. 18. 67-82.

Oliver, R. L. 1997. *Satisfaction: A behavioural perspective on the consumer.* New York: McGraw Hill.

Oliver, R. L. 1980. A cognitive model of the antecedents and consequences of satisfaction Decisions. *Journal of Marketing Research*. 17. 460-470.

Oliver, R. L. 1999. Whence consumer loyalty. *Journal of Marketing*. 4. 33-45.

O'Loughlin C. Coenders, G. 2004. Estimation of the European Customer Satisfaction Index: Maximum Likelihood versus Partial Least Squares. Application to Postal Services. *Total Quality Management & Business Excellence*. 15. 1231-1255.

Parasuraman, A. Zeithaml, V. A. Berry, L. L. 1988. SERVQUAL: A Multiple-Item Scale for Measuring Consumer Perceptions of Service Quality. *Journal of Retailing*. 64. 12-41.

Porter, M.E. 1980. *Competitive Sh-ategy; Techniques for analyzing industries and competitors*. New York: Macmillan

Ramneck, k. Preety, M. 2008. *Telecom fairytale-Customer Loyalty. GNIMT Model Town, Ludhiana.* Available from: http://www.scribd.com/doc/4705254/A-Telecom-fairytaleCustomer-Loyalty.[Accessed May 20, 2010].

Rosenberg, L. Czepiel, J.A. A. 1984. Marketing approach to customer retention. *Journal of Consumer Marketing*. 1. 45-51.

Rundle, T. S. 2005. Elaborating customer loyalty: exploring loyalty to wine retailers. *Journal of Retailing and Consumer Services.* 12. 333-345.

Scitovszky, Tibor. 1945. Some Consequences of the Habit of Judging Quality by Price. *Review of Economic Studies.* 12. 100-105.

Schmidt, L. (2006) Customer Loyalty... Satisfaction has its Rewards. Available from: http://www.marketingwithstyle.com/satisfaction.html [Accessed March 28, 2010].

SCSB: Fornell, C., 1992. A national customer satisfaction barometer: The Swedish experience, *Journal of Marketing*, 56. 6-22.

Selnes, F., 1993. An examination of the effect of product performance on brand reputation, satisfaction and loyalty, *European Journal of Marketing*, 27, 19-35.

Serkan, A., Gokhan O., 2005. The analysis of antecedents of customer loyalty in the Turkish mobile telecommunication market, *European Journal of Marketing*, 39, 910-925.

Shuai, Z., Zhen, L., 2008. How to enhance customer loyalty. *Xi An university. Business Management department. China,* 15 -17.

Soderlund, M., 1998. Customer satisfaction and its consequences on customer behavior revisited. *International Journal of Service Industry Management*, 9, 169-188.

Teas, R. K., 1993. Expectations, performance evaluation, and consumers' perceptions of quality, *Journal of Marketing*, 57,18-35.

Teas, R. K., Agarwal, S., 2000. The Effects of Extrinsic Product Cues on Consumers' Perceptions of Quality, Sacrifice, and Value, *Journal of the Academy of Marketing* Science, 28, 278-291.

Ueltschy, L.C., Laroche, M., Eggert, A., Bindl, U., 2007. Service quality and satisfaction:an international comparison of professional services perceptions. *Journal of Services Marketing*, 21, 410-423

Wang, J. J., 2009. Report of Chinese telecom industry, *Panorama Financial Search* http://search.p5w.net/pdf/Res/CN_RES/INDUS/2009/1/8/c017be7e-9dd7-4f05-b1e7-0560de0d9ed8.pdf [Accessed 22 March 2010].

Woodruff, R.B., 1997. Customer value: The next source for competitive advantage. *Journal of the Academy of Marketing Science*, 25, 139-154.

Xiaoli, X., Yinghong, W., Zhijian, H., Hui, L., 2006. The impact of service quality, satisfaction, value and switching barrier on customer loyalty in Chinese airline industry. *International Conference on Service Systems and Service Management*, 2, 1316-1321.

Yonggui W., Lei D., Shunping H., Guicheng S., 2005. The dimensions of customer loyalty and its key drivers: an integrated framework in perspective of customer equity management, Services Systems and Services Management. Proceedings of ICSSSM '05. *2005 International Conference on*, 1, 204-210.

Yonggui, W., Hing-Po, L., Yongheng, Y., 2004. An integrated framework for service quality, customer value, satisfaction: Evidence from China's telecommunication industry. *Information Systems Frontiers*, 6, 325-340.

Yuksel A., Yuksel F., 2001. Measurement and Management Issues in Customer Satisfaction Research: Review, Critique and Research Agenda: Part One. *Journal of travel and tourism marketing*, 10, 47-80.

Zairi, M, 2000. Managing Customer Dissatisfaction through Effective Complaint management Systems. *The TQM Magazine*,12, 331-335.

Zeithaml, V. A., 1988. Consumer Perceptions of Price, Quality, and Value: A Means-Ends Model and Synthesis of Evidence. *Journal of Marketing*, 52, 2-22.

APPENDIX 1

QUESTIONNAIRE

OBAFEMI AWOLOWO UNIVERSITY
DEPARTMENT OF MANAGEMENT ACCOUNTING

PROMOTING CUSTOMER LOYALTY IN NIGERIA MOBILE
TELECOMMUNICATION INDUSTRY

Dear Respondent,

This questionnaire is designed to study the variables capable of influencing the loyalty of mobile phone users to their preferred operators in Nigeria. This study is part of the requirement for the award of a Master's degree in Business Administration (MBA). Please find time to correctly complete the questionnaire. Your name is not required and information supplied will be treated with utmost confidentiality. Thank you for your cooperation.

Your sincerely
Bello Olayiwola W

Part A: Background information of respondents

1. Gender: i.   [ ] Male   ii.   [ ] Female

2. Age: i.   [ ] 16 - 20   ii.   [ ] 21 - 25   iii.   [ ] 26 - 30
              iv.   [ ] 31 - 35   v.   [ ] above 35

3. Mobile Phone Service Provider
   i.   [ ] MTN   ii   [ ] GLOBACOM
   iii.   [ ] ZAIN   iv.   [ ] ETISALAT

4. How long have you been your current mobile phone network provider?
   i.   [ ] Less than a year   ii.   [ ] One to two years
   iii.   [ ] Three to four years   iv.   [ ] Five years and above

70

Part B: Do you think your loyalty towards your mobile phone network provider can
be influenced by the following factors?

***Note: SA=Strongly Agree; AG=Agree; U=Undecided; D=Disagree; SD=Strongly Agree**

LOYALTY VARIABLES	SA	AG	U	D	SD
Quality of phone call e.g. Call clarity ,connection/ Signal Quality					
Phone network coverage areas					
Quality of SMS (Delivery speed and failure)					
Network quality such as Mobile internet					
The convenience and reliability of customer service call					
The service quality of Service Centre					
Rating price of given quality					
Score accumulation plan and bonus Mileage program (free call, free SMS as bonus or awards)					
Be afraid of troubles after changing your cell phone number					
Advertisements about corporate image e.g. Brand image					
Others (Please Specify)					

12. **Amongst the 11 influencing factors above, which are the main factors you are really concerned about when deciding to be loyal to one specific brand/company? (Tick as many as applicable)**

[   ] Call quality   [   ] Coverage of area
[   ] Quality of SMS   [   ] The service quality of service center
[   ] Rating price of given quality   [   ] Advertisements such as Brand image
[   ] Social responsibility   [   ] Network quality e.g. Value-added services
[   ] Worry of troubles after changing phone number
[   ] Convenience and reliability of customer service call
[   ] Loss of benefits of score accumulation and bonus (free call, free SMS as bonus or awards)

Part C: Are you satisfied with the performance of your service provider in the following areas?

***NOTE VS=Very Satisfied; SA=Satisfied; U=Undecided; US=Unsatisfied; VU=Very Unsatisfied**

PROVIDER'S PERFORMANCE ON LOYALTY VARIABLES	VS	SA	U	US	VU
Quality of phone call					
The coverage of area					
Quality of SMS					
Internet Service					
Convenience and reliability of customer service call					
Service quality of Service Centre					
Rating Price of Given quality					
Have you joined any commercial promotional activities held by your service provider?(Tariff plan)					
For the ones that you have joined, are you satisfied with them?					
Are you satisfied with advertisements of your service provider?					
Are you satisfied with the attitudes and performances of your service provider on taking social responsibility?					
In General, are you satisfied with your service provider?					

13   Will you recommend your family or friends to the telecom service of your service provider you are currently using?
[   ] Yes   [   ] No